JOHN GRAY

Seven Types of Atheism

PENGUIN BOOKS

PENGUIN BOOKS

UK | USA | Canada | Ireland | Australia
India | New Zealand | South Africa

Penguin Books is part of the Penguin Random House group of companies
whose addresses can be found at global.penguinrandomhouse.com.

First published by Allen Lane 2018
Published in Penguin Books 2019
001

Copyright © John Gray, 2018
The moral right of the author has been asserted

Set in 9.26/12.36 pt Sabon LT Std
Typeset by Jouve (UK), Milton Keynes
Printed and bound in Great Britain by Clays Ltd, Elcograf S.p.A.

A CIP catalogue record for this book is available from the British Library

ISBN: 978-0-141-98110-9

www.greenpenguin.co.uk

Contents

Introduction: How to be an Atheist

Contemporary atheism is a flight from a godless world. Life without any power that can secure order or some kind of ultimate justice is a frightening and for many an intolerable prospect. In the absence of such a power, human events could be finally chaotic, and no story could be told that satisfied the need for meaning. Struggling to escape this vision, atheists have looked for surrogates of the God they have cast aside. The progress of humanity has replaced belief in divine providence. But this faith in humanity makes sense only if it continues ways of thinking that have been inherited from monotheism. The idea that the human species realizes common goals throughout history is a secular avatar of a religious idea of redemption.

Atheism has not always been like this. Along with many who have searched for a surrogate Deity to fill the hole left by the God that has departed, there have been some who stepped out of monotheism altogether and in doing so found freedom and fulfilment. Not looking for cosmic meaning, they were content with the world as they found it.

By no means all atheists have wanted to convert others to their view of things. Some have been friendly to traditional faiths, preferring the worship of a God they think fictitious to a religion of humanity. Most atheists today are liberals, who believe the species is slowly making its way towards a better world; but modern liberalism is a late flower of Jewish and Christian religion, and in the past most atheists have not been liberals. Some atheists have gloried in the majesty of the cosmos. Others have delighted in the small worlds human beings make for themselves.

While atheists may call themselves freethinkers, for many today atheism is a closed system of thought. That may be its chief attraction. When you explore older atheisms, you will find that some of your firmest convictions – secular or religious – are highly questionable. If this prospect disturbs you, what you are looking for may be freedom from thinking. But if you are ready to leave behind the needs and hopes that many atheists have carried over from monotheism, you may find that a burden has been lifted from you. Some older atheisms are oppressive and claustrophobic, like much of atheism at the present time. Others can be refreshing and liberating for anyone who wants a new perspective on the world. Paradoxically, some of the most radical forms of atheism may in the end be not so different from some mystical varieties of religion.

Defining atheism is like trying to capture the diversity of religions in a formula. Following the poet, critic and impassioned atheist William Empson, I will suggest it is an essential part of terms like 'religion' and 'atheism' that they can have multiple meanings. Neither religion nor atheism has anything like an essence. Borrowing an analogy from the Austrian-British philosopher Ludwig Wittgenstein, they are more like extended families, which display recognizable similarities without having any single feature in common. This view inspired the American pragmatist William James to write *The Varieties of Religious Experience*, the best book ever written on religion by a philosopher and one that Wittgenstein much admired.

A provisional definition of atheism might still be useful, if only to indicate the drift of the book that follows. So I suggest that an atheist is anyone with no use for the idea of a divine mind that has fashioned the world. In this sense atheism does not amount to very much. It is simply the absence of the idea of a creator-god.

There is precedent for thinking of atheism in these terms. In the ancient European world atheism meant the refusal to participate in traditional practices honouring the gods of the polytheistic pantheon. Christians were described as 'atheists' (in Greek *atheos*, meaning 'without gods') because they worshipped only one god. Then as now, atheism and monotheism were sides of the same coin.

If you think of atheism in this way you will see that it is not the same as the rejection of religion. For most human beings religion has always consisted of practices more than beliefs. When Christians in the Roman Empire were required to follow the Roman religion (*religio* in Latin), this meant observing Roman ceremonies. These included acts of worship to pagan gods, but nothing was demanded in terms of belief. The word 'pagan' (*pagani*) is a Christian invention applied in the early fourth century to those who followed these practices.[1] 'Paganism' was not a creed – the people described as pagans had no concept of heresy, for one thing – but a jumble of observances.

A provisional definition of religion may also be useful. Many of the practices that are recognized as religious express a need to make sense of the human passage through the world. 'Birth, and copulation, and death' may be all there is in the end. As Sweeney says in T. S. Eliot's *Fragment of an Agon* – 'That's all the facts when you come to brass tacks.' But human beings have been reluctant to accept this, and struggle to bestow some more-than-human significance on their lives. Tribal animists and practitioners of world faiths, devotees of flying-saucer cults and the armies of zealots that have killed and died for modern secular faiths attest to this need for meaning. With its reverent invocation of the progress of the species, the evangelical unbelief of recent times obeys the same impulse. Religion is an attempt to find meaning in events, not a theory that tries to explain the universe.

Rather than atheism being a worldview that recurs throughout history, there have been many atheisms with conflicting views of the world. In ancient Greece and Rome, India and China there were schools of thought that, without denying that gods existed, were convinced they were not concerned with humans. Some of these schools developed early versions of the philosophy which holds that everything in the world is composed of matter. Others held back from speculating about the nature of things. The Roman poet Lucretius thought the universe was composed of 'atoms and the void', whereas the Chinese mystic Chuang Tzu followed the (possibly mythical) Taoist sage Lao Tzu in thinking the world had a way of working that could not be grasped by human reason. Since their view of things did not contain a divine mind that created the universe, both were atheists. But neither of them fussed about 'the existence of God', since they had no conception of a creator-god to question or reject.

Religion is universal, whereas monotheism is a local cult. Many 'primitive' cultures contain elaborate creation myths – stories of how the world came into being. Some tell of it emerging from a primordial chaos, others of it springing from a cosmic egg, still others of it arising from the dismembered parts of a dead god. But few of these stories feature a god that fashioned the universe. There may be gods or spirits, but they are not supernatural. In animism, the original religion of all humankind, the natural world is thick with spirits.

Just as not all religions contain the idea of a creator-god, there have been many without any idea of an immortal soul. In some religions – such as those that produced Norse mythology – the gods themselves are mortal. Greek polytheists expected an afterlife, but believed it would be populated by the shades of people who had once existed, not these people in a posthumous form. Biblical Judaism conceived of an underworld (Sheol) in much the same way. Jesus promised his disciples salvation from death, but through the resurrection of their fleshly bodies, divinely perfected. There have been atheists who believed human personality continues after bodily death. In Victorian and Edwardian times, some psychical researchers thought an afterlife meant passing into another part of the natural world.

If there are many different religions, there are also many different atheisms. Twenty-first-century atheism is nearly always a type of materialism. But that is only one of many views of the world that atheists have held. Some atheists – such as the nineteenth-century German philosopher Arthur Schopenhauer – have thought that matter is an illusion and reality spiritual. There is no such thing as 'the atheist worldview'. Atheism simply excludes the idea that the world is the work of a creator-god, which is not found in most religions.

WHAT RELIGION IS NOT

The idea that religion is a matter of belief is parochial. What did Homer 'believe'? Or the authors of the *Bhagavad-Gita*? The web of traditions that western scholars have described as 'Hinduism' comes with no prescribed creed, any more than does the mixture of folk religion with mysticism that western scholars call 'Taoism'.

The notion that religions are creeds – lists of propositions or doctrines that everyone must accept or reject – emerged only with Christianity. Belief was never as important as observance in Jewish religion. In its earliest biblical forms, the religion practised by the Jewish people was a type not of monotheism – the assertion that there is only one God – but of henotheism, the exclusive worship of their own God. Worshipping foreign gods was condemned as disloyalty, not as unbelief. It was only some time around the sixth century BC, during the period when the Israelites returned from exile to Jerusalem, that the idea that there is only one God emerged in Jewish religion. Even then the heart of Judaism continued to be practice, not belief.

Christianity has been a religion of belief from the time it was invented. But there have been Christian traditions in which belief is not central. Eastern Orthodoxy holds that God is beyond any human conception – a view fleshed out in what is known as negative or apophatic theology. Even in western Christianity, 'believing in God' has not always meant asserting the existence of a supernatural being. The thirteenth-century Catholic theologian Thomas Aquinas (1225–74) was explicit that God does not exist in the same way that any particular thing exists.

In most religions, debates about belief are unimportant. Belief was irrelevant in pagan religion and continues to be unimportant in the religions of India and China. When they declare themselves unbelievers, atheists are invoking an understanding of religion that has been unthinkingly inherited from monotheism.

Many religions that feature a creator-god have imagined it very differently from the God that has been worshipped in Judaism, Christianity and Islam. Since the rise of Christianity the divine mind that is supposed to have created the world has often been conceived as being perfectly good. However, Gnostic traditions have envisioned a supreme God that created the universe and then withdrew into itself, leaving the world to be ruled by a lesser god, or Demiurge, which might be indifferent or hostile to humankind. Such Gnostic ideas may seem to us far-fetched. But they have some advantages over more traditional conceptions of a Supreme Being. For one thing, they resolve the 'problem of evil'. If God is all powerful and all good, why is there evil in the world? A familiar response has it that evil is required by free will, without which there can be no true goodness. This is the central claim of Christian theodicy (in Greek, 'justifying God') – the attempt to explain evil as part of a divine design. An entire tradition of atheism has developed against theodicy, memorably articulated by Ivan Karamazov, who in Dostoevsky's novel *The Brothers Karamazov* declares that if a tortured child is the price of goodness then he will hand back to God his entry ticket to the world. I consider this type of atheism – sometimes called misotheism, or God-hatred – in Chapter 5.

Taking monotheism as a model for religion is misleading. It is not only animism and polytheism that are left out of the picture. Nontheist religions are ignored as well. Buddhism says nothing of any divine mind and rejects any idea of the soul. The world consists of processes and events. The human sense of self is an illusion; freedom is found in ridding oneself of this illusion. Popular Buddhism has retained ideas of the transmigration of souls that were current in India at the time when the Buddha lived, along with the belief that merits accumulated in one life can be passed on to another. But the idea of karma, which underpins these beliefs, denotes an impersonal process of cause and effect rather than reward or punishment by a Supreme Being. Nowhere does Buddhism speak of such a Being, and it is in fact an atheist religion. The smears and fulminations of the 'new atheists' make sense only in a specifically Christian context, and even then only within a few subsets of the Christian religion.

SEVEN TYPES OF ATHEISM

In his book *Seven Types of Ambiguity* (1930), Empson – whose own version of atheism I discuss in Chapter 5 – showed how language could be open-ended without being misleading. Ambiguity, he suggested, is not a defect but part of the richness of language. Rather than signifying equivocation or confusion, ambiguous expressions allow us to describe a fluid and paradoxical world.

Empson applied this account of ambiguity chiefly to poetry, but it is also illuminating when applied to religion and atheism. Describing ambiguity as 'any verbal nuance, however slight, which gives room for alternative reactions to the same piece of language', he observed that 'any prose statement could be called ambiguous'. There could be no such thing as ultimate clarity. 'One can do a great deal to make poetry intelligible', Empson wrote, 'by discussing the resultant variety of meanings.'[2] It was the nuances of meaning that made poetry possible. In a later book, *The Structure of Complex Words* (1951), Empson showed how the most straightforward-looking terms were 'compacted with doctrines' that left their meaning equivocal. There is no hidden simplicity concealed by complex words. Inherently plural in meaning, words enable different ways of seeing the world.

Applying Empson's method, I will examine seven kinds of atheism. The first of them – the so-called 'new atheism' – contains little that is novel or interesting. After the first chapter, I will not refer to it again. The second type is secular humanism, a hollowed-out version of the Christian belief in salvation in history. Third, there is the kind of atheism that makes a religion from science, a category that includes evolutionary humanism, Mesmerism, dialectical materialism and contemporary transhumanism. Fourth, there are modern political religions, from Jacobinism through communism and Nazism to contemporary evangelical liberalism. Fifth, there is the atheism of God-haters such as the Marquis de Sade, Dostoevsky's fictional character Ivan Karamazov and William Empson himself. Sixth, I will consider the atheisms of George Santayana and Joseph Conrad, which reject the idea of a creator-god without having any piety towards 'humanity'. Seventh and last, there are the mystical atheism of Arthur Schopenhauer and the negative theologies of Benedict Spinoza and the early twentieth-century Russian-Jewish fideist Leo Shestov, all of which in different ways point to a God that transcends any human conception.

I have no interest in converting anyone to or from any of these types of atheism. But my own preferences will be clear. Repelled by the first five varieties I am drawn to the last two, atheisms that are happy to live with a godless world or an unnameable God.

I

The New Atheism: A Nineteenth-century Orthodoxy

The new atheists have directed their campaign against a narrow segment of religion while failing to understand even that small part. Seeing religion as a system of beliefs, they have attacked it as if it was no more than an obsolete scientific theory. Hence the 'God debate' – a tedious re-run of a Victorian squabble between science and religion. But the idea that religion consists of a bunch of discredited theories is itself a discredited theory – a relic of the nineteenth-century philosophy of Positivism.

THE GRAND PONTIFF OF HUMANITY

The idea that religion is a primitive sort of science was popularized by the anthropologist J. G. Frazer in *The Golden Bough: a study in comparative religion*, which first appeared in 1890. Following the French sociologist and philosopher Auguste Comte, Frazer believed that human thought developed in three phases: the theological, or religious, the metaphysical-philosophical, or abstract, and the scientific, or positive. Magic, metaphysics and theology belonged in the infancy of the species. As it approached adulthood humankind would shed them and accept science as the only authority in knowledge and ethics.

This way of thinking, which Comte called 'the Positive philosophy', developed some of the ideas of Henri de Saint-Simon (1760–1825), for whom Comte for a time acted as an assistant. Saint-Simon led a turbulent life. Coming from an impoverished aristocratic family, he was imprisoned during the Reign of Terror, became rich through property speculation in nationalized land, consumed his wealth in reckless extravagance and lived much of his later years in poverty. Like his disciple Comte he was prone to depression, at one point attempting suicide by shooting himself but succeeding only in blinding himself in one eye.

Despite these eccentricities Saint-Simon was widely admired. Recognized by Marx as one of the founding theorists of socialism, he was among the first to understand that industrialization would bring about radical changes in society. He was also the first to set out, in his book *Nouveau Christianisme* (1825), the religion of humanity that Comte would promote.

This new faith was not Saint-Simon's invention. As will be seen in Chapters 2 and 3, it emerged in the late eighteenth century in the work of the French *philosophes* and became overtly religious in the cult of reason in the aftermath of the French Revolution. But it was Saint-Simon who first presented the religion of humanity in systematic form. In future, scientists would replace priests as the spiritual leaders of society. Government would be an easy matter of 'the administration of things'. Religion would become the self-worship of humankind.

Though it was Saint-Simon who first formulated this philosophy, it was Comte who was most successful in propagating it. The cult he established has been almost forgotten. Yet it formed the template for the secular humanism that all evangelical atheists promote today.

In some ways Comte was more intelligent than the secular thinkers who followed him. He was also semi-deranged. Recognizing that the need for religion would not wither away when society was governed by science, he founded a church to meet this need. The new faith was equipped with an ecclesiastical hierarchy, a calendar organized around figures such as Archimedes and Descartes, a regime of daily observances (including a ritual that involved tapping parts of the cranium based on the popular science of phrenology) and a Virgin Mother modelled on a married woman with whom Comte had fallen in love and from whose untimely death he never fully recovered.

In his book *Cathechisme Positiviste* (1852), Comte set out the dogmas of the new creed. There were Positivist sacraments and places of pilgrimage. Special types of clothing were designed, with buttons placed on the back so that they could not be worn without the help of others – thereby promoting altruism (a word Comte invented). A Grand Pontiff of Humanity was to be established in Paris. No doubt Comte envisioned occupying the position himself. Certainly he imagined himself a person of some importance. In the ceremony in which he married his wife, he signed himself 'Brutus Napoleon Comte'. During his lifetime (born in 1798, he died of cancer in 1857) he failed to achieve the eminence of which he dreamt. But his church spread from France to Britain and other European countries, then to Latin America, where it continues to exist in Brazil, while his philosophy had a profound impact on leading nineteenth-century thinkers. It continues to have a pervasive though unrecognized influence today.

The new atheists are unwitting disciples of Comte's Positivist philosophy. It seems self-evident to them that religion is a primitive sort of science. But this is itself a primitive view, and a remark made by Wittgenstein about Frazer applies equally to Richard Dawkins and his followers: 'Frazer is much more savage than most of his savages ... *His* explanations of primitive practices are much cruder than the meaning of these practices themselves.'[1]

The primitive character of the new atheism shows itself in the notion that religions are erroneous hypotheses. The Genesis story is not an early theory of the origin of species. In the fourth century AD the founding theologian of western Christianity St Augustine devoted fifteen years to composing a treatise on *The Literal Meaning of Genesis*, never completed, in which he argued that the biblical text need not be understood literally if it goes against what we know to be true from other sources. Before Augustine, and more radically, the first-century Greek-speaking Jewish philosopher Philo of Alexandria presented Genesis as an allegory or myth – an interweaving of symbolic imagery with imagined events that contained a body of meaning that could not easily be expressed in other ways.

The story of Adam and Eve eating from the Tree of Knowledge is a mythical imagining of the ambiguous impact of knowledge on human freedom. Rather than being inherently liberating, knowledge can be used for purposes of enslavement. That is what is meant when, having eaten the forbidden apple after the serpent promises them they will become like gods, Adam and Eve find themselves exiled from the Garden of Eden and condemned to a life of unceasing labour. Unlike scientific theories, myths cannot be true or false. But myths can be more or less truthful to human experience. The Genesis myth is a more truthful rendition of enduring human conflicts than anything in Greek philosophy, which is founded on the myth that knowledge and goodness are inseparably connected.

Part of the blame for the confusion of myths with theories comes from theists peddling an Argument from Design. From the eighteenth-century English theologian William Paley (who famously compared God to a clock-maker) to twenty-first-century exponents of creationism, apologists for theism have tried to develop theories that explain the origins of the universe and humankind better than prevailing scientific accounts. In doing so they are conceding to science an unwarranted authority over other ways of thinking. Religion is no more a primitive type of science than is art or poetry. Scientific inquiry answers a demand for explanation. The practice of religion expresses a need for meaning, which would remain unsatisfied even if everything could be explained.

WHY SCIENCE CANNOT DISPEL RELIGION

Science cannot replace a religious view of the world, since there is no such thing as 'the scientific worldview'. A method of inquiry rather than a settled body of theories, science yields different views of the world as knowledge advances. Until Darwin showed that species change over time, science pictured a world of fixed species. In the same way, classical physics has been followed by quantum mechanics. It is commonly assumed that science will someday yield a single unchanging view of things. Certainly some views of the world are eliminated as scientific knowledge advances. But there is no reason for supposing that the progress of science will reach a point where only one worldview is left standing.

Some will stay this is tantamount to relativism – the claim that views of the world are only cultural constructions, none of them true or false. Against this philosophy, it is asserted that science is the exercise of discovering universal laws of nature. But unless you believe the human mind mirrors a rational cosmos – the faith of Plato and the Stoics, which helped shape Christianity – science can only be a tool the human animal has invented to deal with a world it cannot fully understand. No doubt our knowledge has increased, and will continue to increase. But the order that appears to prevail in our corner of the universe may be local and ephemeral, emerging randomly and then melting away. The very idea that we live in a law-governed cosmos may be not much more than a fading legacy of faith in a divine law-giver.

Above all, science cannot dispel religion by showing it to be an illusion. The rationalist philosophy according to which religion is an intellectual error is fundamentally at odds with scientific inquiry into religion as a natural human activity. Religion may involve the creation of illusions. But there is nothing in science that says illusion may not be useful, even indispensable, in life. The human mind is programmed for survival, not truth. Rather than producing minds that see the world ever more clearly, evolution could have the effect of breeding any clear view of things out of the mind. The upshot of scientific inquiry could be that a need for illusion goes with being human. The recurring appearance of religions of science suggests this may in fact be the case.

Atheists who think of religions as erroneous theories mistake faith – trust in an unknown power – for belief. But if there is a problem with belief, it is not confined to religion. Much of what passes as scientific knowledge is as open to doubt as the miraculous events that feature in traditional faiths. Wander among the shelves of the social sciences stacks in university libraries, and you find yourself in a mausoleum of dead theories. These theories have not passed into the intellectual netherworld by being falsified. Most are not even false; they are too nebulous to allow empirical testing. Systems of ideas such as Positivism and Marxism that forecast the decline of religion have been confounded time and time again. Yet these cod-scientific speculations linger on in a dim afterlife in the minds of many who have never heard of the ideas from which they sprang.

If Comte's nineteenth-century cult of science produced an ersatz religion joined with the pseudo-science of phrenology, Dawkins and his disciples have embellished Darwinism with the cod-science of memes – units of information that compete for survival in a process of natural selection like that which operates on genes. But memes are not physical entities like genes. No mechanism has been identified whereby memes could replicate themselves and be transmitted within or across cultures. Lacking any unit or mechanism of selection, the theory of memes is barely a theory at all.

The idea of memes belongs in an obsolete philosophy of language. The early Wittgenstein imagined that language could be broken down into 'logical atoms', elementary propositions that refer to irreducibly simple facts about the world. But he was never able to provide an example of such an atom – a failing which led him to his later philosophy in which language is understood as a body of interconnected practices. Memes are like Wittgenstein's logical atoms, theoretical constructions of which no convincing examples can be found. Is Romanticism a meme? Or the Middle Ages? Genes can be identified by well-established scientific procedures, memes cannot. As insubstantial as phlogiston, memes are posited only in order to bolster the belief that evolution can explain everything.

Whenever it has appeared as an organized movement in modern times, atheism has always allied itself with pseudo-science. Dawkins's memes belong in the same category as the bumps on the head that Comte instructed his disciples to tap as part of the daily observances of the religion of humanity.

THE TRUE THREAT TO MONOTHEISM

The Victorian debate between science and religion is best forgotten. A more serious challenge to Christianity comes from history. If Jesus was not crucified and did not return from the dead the Christian religion is seriously compromised. The same is true if what Jesus taught was other than Christians later came to believe.

The real conflict is not between religion and science but between Christianity and history. The Christian religion rests on the belief that human salvation is bound up with particular historical events – the life, death and resurrection of Jesus. Religions such as Hinduism, Buddhism, Taoism and the innumerable varieties of polytheism all contain stories of what would now be seen as miracles. But these religions do not depend on such stories being accepted as literally true, whereas Christianity is liable to falsification by historical fact.

It is a difficulty that cannot be avoided by placing the story of Jesus in the category of the Genesis myth. Adam and Eve's expulsion from paradise will remain one of humankind's most instructive myths however much scientific understanding of human origins advances. In contrast, Christianity will be badly shaken if the received story of Jesus can be shown to be false. Jewish and Christian scholars have recognized for millennia that the Genesis story is not a rendition of fact. The New Testament account of the life of Jesus has been reported as fact ever since the Christian religion was invented.

Investigations of the historical Jesus have gone through a number of phases. The eighteenth-century German Enlightenment thinker Hermann Samuel Reimarus began the inquiry with a study, not published in his lifetime, in which he pictured Jesus as a revolutionary Jewish prophet who failed to achieve his goals and died in despair on the cross, leaving his disciples with a dilemma they resolved by telling a story of his resurrection that they knew to be groundless. The search for the historical Jesus was continued by the nineteenth-century German David Strauss, whose work sparked a controversy as intense and as long-lasting as that triggered by Darwin's writings. Arguing that the life of Jesus should be understood without any recourse to miracles, Strauss suggested that the view of him accepted by Christians was a myth fashioned by Jesus' disciples. The work of Reimarus and Strauss initiated many later studies, including Albert Schweitzer's *The Quest of the Historical Jesus* (1906) in which Jesus was portrayed as a Jewish prophet the heart of whose teaching was the belief that the world was about to end. The quest has continued into recent times, featuring seminal studies such as Géza Vermes's *The Changing Faces of Jesus* (2000).

While much of this inquiry has involved textual criticism of the four gospels of the New Testament, more recent inquiries have taken into account texts such as the Dead Sea Scrolls, discovered in the late 1940s in caves near the ancient settlement of Qumran on the north-west shore of the Dead Sea. The implications of these texts are disputed, with Christian scholars attempting to defuse the threat the texts pose to the accepted picture of Jesus and his teachings. Yet the clear upshot is that the story of Jesus that has been told by Christians is only one of many that can reasonably be told about him.

In one plausible account, Jesus was not the founder of Christianity. A charismatic Jewish teacher (Yeshua in Hebrew) who joined a movement led by John the Baptist, he was one of many itinerant Jewish prophets preaching at the time. He had no message for Gentiles and no idea of founding a universal religion. He did not claim to be the messiah prophesied in the Old Testament, still less a saviour for all of humankind. His religion was that of Moses applied in what he believed were the final days of the world. He expected the arrival of the 'day of the Lord' (in Greek, *eschaton*) to occur during his life-time. The morality he taught his disciples was what Schweitzer called an *Interimsethik* – a way of life meant for the short period before the advent of the kingdom of God. There was no mention of free will; the world was about to end whatever anyone did. The idea of an immortal soul was nowhere to be found. In the religion of Jesus, pretty much all of Christian belief is absent.

Above all, the kingdom of heaven that Jesus announced was meant for Jews like himself. He may have accepted the message of the Book of Isaiah, which suggests that Gentiles could follow Jews into God's Kingdom. Even so Jesus' mission was addressed only to other Jews. So how did this charismatic Jewish prophet come to be seen as the saviour of humankind?

Following Jesus' crucifixion, the advent of a new world during his lifetime could no longer be expected. When he failed to return from the grave the shock to his disciples must have been overwhelming. Their response was that a Second Coming would soon occur. This was the message of the apostle Paul, a Greek-speaking Jew and Roman citizen also known as Saul of Tarsus, in letters composed only twenty years after Jesus' death. By the time of the New Testament gospel of John, probably produced towards the end of the first century AD, Jesus had become the Son of God – not a human being but part of the Deity. Later, the kingdom of God that Jesus expected was interpreted as meaning a spiritual realm that existed out of time, an idea developed by St Augustine, a convert from Manicheism who in the fourth century AD melded Jesus' teachings with the Greek philosophy of Platonism.

Paul and Augustine invented the religion we know as Christianity. From them comes an obsession with sexuality that has no precedent in the extant teaching of Jesus. In his *Confessions*, Augustine records that in his youth he would pray, 'God, make me chaste – but not yet.' A view of sexual desire as sanctioned in wedlock but otherwise sinful was an integral part of the Christian religion from Paul onwards. Ever after, the idea of original sin shaped most forms of Christianity, though it has not been central in Eastern Orthodoxy.

Augustine demanded that Christianity make a radical breach with the Jewish heritage of Jesus. 'The true image of the Hebrew', he wrote in *Tractatus adversus Judaeos* (*Treatise against the Jews*), 'is Judas Iscariot, who sells the Lord for silver. The Jews can never understand scripture, and forever bear the guilt of the death of Christ.' The accusation that Jews killed Jesus had been made earlier by St Paul in his first letter to the Thessalonians (2:14–15). It was Paul who was pivotal in turning an exclusively Jewish movement into one that not only accepted Gentiles but actively attempted to convert them.

Because salvation was no longer open only to a particular people as in Judaism, or a few initiates as in Greco-Roman mystery cults, Christianity is commonly regarded as an improvement on the religions of the ancient world. But the price of universal hope was evangelical belief. The faith that Jesus asked from his disciples did not mean accepting a creed. It meant trusting in him. He did not teach a set of principles but showed his followers a way of living. Containing little or nothing of theology, his gospel was concerned with deeds, not words. From Paul onwards, he became the central icon in a cult of belief. From being a prophet, he became God on earth. What had been a way of life was turned into a missionary ideology, with all of humankind being in need of conversion. The scene was set for millennia of conflict. Christians invented the idea of religion as it is commonly understood today. Rejecting the traditions of the ancient world as worship of false gods, they for the first time identified faith with belief. This equation is the chief source of the doctrinal violence that has ravaged western civilization ever since.

At the same time, by remaking religion as a form of belief – a matter of conscience, not just ritual observance – Christianity created a demand for freedom that did not exist in the ancient world. Valuing inward worship more than public practice, the early Christians set in motion a movement that would culminate in the creation of a secular realm. Even as it planted violence in the heart of religion, Christianity sowed the seed of the separation of Church and state. Here Christians followed the teaching of Jesus, who instructed his disciples to render unto Caesar the things that are Caesar's and unto God those that are God's (Matthew 22:21).

On the basis of available evidence, Jesus was most likely a Jewish prophet in the tradition of John the Baptist. But other accounts of his life and teachings cannot be ruled out. He may have been a Zealot who led a Jewish revolt against the Romans after which he was crucified and did not rise from the grave. He may have belonged to a Jewish school of Cynicism, the philosophy associated with the fourth-century BC Greek sage Diogenes, who taught indifference to conventional values. He may have sprung from the Essene movement, a dissident Jewish sect that practised an ascetic form of communal living not unlike that of later Christian monasticism.

In other accounts, Jesus may have married, divorced and re-married, spent some years preaching his gospel and died a natural death. He may have been a rabbi from a prosperous family, who gave up a comfortable life in order to become a wandering teacher of the inner meaning of Jewish law. His original apostles may have included fishermen, but they may have been reasonably well off until they accepted Jesus' teaching and gave up their worldly goods. Many of Jesus' early followers may have been not outcasts but relatively privileged people. Many versions of Jesus and his life can be supported on the basis of existing evidence. Among the least plausible are those that have been presented as fact by Christian churches.

Christian thinkers have interpreted the rise of their religion as a sign of Jesus' divine nature. Among the many prophets teaching at the time, why should he alone have inspired a religion that spread to the last corner of the earth? It is true that the personality and teaching of Jesus are distinctive. A furious enemy of injustice who preached forgiveness of sins, he stands out from other Jewish prophets of his time. But unless you think that human events unfold under some sort of divine guidance, the metamorphosis of Jesus' teaching into a universal faith can only have been the result of a succession of accidents.

If Paul had not been converted, the movement Jesus founded would most likely never have become a world religion. If the emperor Constantine had not adopted Christianity and Theodosius had not made it the official state religion in the fourth century AD, the Roman world could have continued to be polytheistic. The rise of Christianity was far from inevitable. Between the conversion of Paul and that of Constantine many cults were contending, none of them pre-ordained to prevail over the rest. European culture might well have been shaped by mystery religions like the cults of Mithras, Hermes and Orpheus, while the Christian religion dwindled away and eventually died out. Or some version of Christianity unrecognizably different from the ones with which we are familiar could have triumphed. There were many ancient Christianities, melding with and morphing from Judaism, Manicheism, Gnosticism, Platonism and other traditions. As we know it today, the Christian religion is a creation of chance.

NEW ATHEISM AND OLD ILLIBERALISM

Religions seem substantial and enduring only because they are always invisibly changing. Atheists have used this fact as a weapon against religion. In *An Atheist's Values* (1964), an almost forgotten book that may be the best defence of an atheist ethics ever published, the Oxford philosopher Richard Robinson wrote:

We often hear talk of 'Christian values'. Those who use this phrase are confident that everyone knows what Christian values are. But I do not know what they are. For example, I am puzzled whether thrift is a Christian value in view of the fact that, whereas thrift is often praised by people calling themselves Christians, it is rejected by Jesus in the gospels.[2]

Robinson was right in pointing out that what are described as Christian values are often contradicted by what is known of the teaching of Jesus. He was also right in making clear that the values he defended in his book could not be derived from atheism. They were *his* values – not purely personal preferences, since reasons could be given in support of them, but not necessary features of atheism either. He never claimed there was anything 'objective' or 'scientific' about them.

Atheists attack Christian values because they are changeable and often contradictory. In incessant mawkish debates, they insist that unbelievers can be highly moral people. It does not occur to them to ask *which morality* an atheist should follow. Like Robinson's Christians, they are confident that everyone knows what atheist values must be.

In this as in so much else, they are mistaken. Karl Marx and the Russian anarchist Mikhail Bakunin rejected theism because it was an obstacle to human solidarity, the German egoist Max Stirner because it restricted individual self-assertion and Friedrich Nietzsche because it promoted 'slave virtues' like humility. Some eighteenth-century French atheists such as the physician La Mettrie, whose materialist philosophy is discussed in Chapter 5 when I consider the thought of the Marquis de Sade, recommended the enjoyment of sensual pleasures. Most English atheists at the time and later were horrified by any defence of sensuality. The mid-Victorian philosopher John Stuart Mill looked forward to a time when Christianity would be replaced by something like Comte's religion of humanity. But Mill shared with the Christians of his time the conviction that life should be devoted to mental and moral self-improvement rather than to enjoyment of physical pleasures. There have been many atheist moralities.

With few exceptions, twenty-first-century atheists are unthinking liberals. But atheism has no specific political content, and many atheists have been virulently anti-liberal. Eighteenth-century French *philosophes* – including Voltaire, as we will see – endorsed views that can only be described as racist. Charles Maurras, the early twentieth-century French atheist and chief theorist of the fascistic Action Française movement, revered the Catholic Church as a bastion of social order. The nineteenth-century biologist Ernst Haeckel, who was hailed as 'the German Darwin', invented an evolutionary religion called Monism in which ideas of racial hierarchy played a prominent part. Julian Huxley, one of the founding fathers of 'evolutionary humanism' in twentieth-century Britain, endorsed similar racial theories before the Second World War. Typically, exponents of 'scientific ethics' have merely endorsed the conventional values of their time.

Our time is no different. The American new atheist Sam Harris wants 'a science of good and evil'. He assumes that this science will support liberal values of human equality and personal autonomy. Why it should do so is never explained. Many value-systems have claimed the authority of science. For many advocates of a 'scientific ethics' in the inter-war years of the last century, liberal values were redundant in the communist (or Nazi) future they believed to be imminent.

The project of a scientific ethics is an inheritance from Comte, who believed that once ethics had become a science liberal values would be obsolete. In a rational society, value-judgements would be left to scientific experts. Atheist illiberalism of this kind is one of the strongest currents in modern thought. The more hostile secular thinking is to Jewish and Christian religion, the less likely it is to be liberal. Though he may consider himself a liberal, Harris belongs in this illiberal tradition.

It is not by accident that neither he nor any of the new atheists promotes tolerance as a central value. If ethics can be a science, there is no need for toleration. In fact all these versions of 'scientific ethics' are fraudulent, and not only because the sciences they invoke are bogus. Science cannot close the gap between facts and values. No matter how much it may advance, scientific inquiry cannot tell you which ends to pursue or how to resolve conflicts between them.

Believing that 'the link between morality and happiness seems straightforward', Harris revives a familiar type of Utilitarian ethics in which the only things that have intrinsic value are the pleasures and pains of sentient creatures. It is a long-familiar theory with no less familiar difficulties. How is the value of pleasures and pains to be measured or compared? The founder of Utilitarianism, the early nineteenth-century philosopher and legal reformer Jeremy Bentham, suggested a number of criteria, including duration and intensity. But should pleasures that most people would condemn as bad – the pleasures of cruelty, for example – count equally with others of the same duration and intensity? Bentham thought so, but few have followed him in this view. Again, Harris assumes that Utilitarianism supports the priority liberals give to freedom over other goods. But does it? John Stuart Mill, the greatest exponent of liberal Utilitarianism to date, devoted his famous essay *On Liberty* (1859) to arguing that it did. The end-result of a massive philosophical literature is that Mill's argument failed. Utilitarianism and liberalism are distinct positions, with conflicting implications that cannot always be reconciled.

Harris's ethical stance betrays signs of this conflict. He has endorsed liberal values of freedom and human dignity. At the same time he has defended the practice of torture as being not only permissible but necessary in what he describes as 'our war on terror'. Even if it violates basic freedoms, he argues, torture may protect freedom on balance. Reasonable people may have different responses to this claim, some thinking it betrays core liberal values, others that it reveals the conflicts these values face in practice. But, either way, science cannot decide whether or when torture can be justified.

The reason Harris passes over these questions is not only a lack of knowledge on his part. By cultivating a willed ignorance of the history of ideas, he is able to avoid noticing that atheism and illiberalism have often been bedfellows. He can then pass over the fact that the liberal values he claims to profess originated in monotheism.

In itself negative, atheism has inspired many secular creeds. When it has been promoted in organized movements it has acquired the trappings of traditional religions. From the Religion of Reason that developed in the course of the French Revolution through Comte's religion of humanity and Haeckel's Monism, Lenin's dialectical materialism and Ayn Rand's reinvention of Nietzsche's superman, atheist movements have been vehicles for surrogate religions.

At the same time as it has spawned ersatz religion, evangelical atheism has fuelled faith-based politics. During the French Revolution places of worship were ransacked and wrecked in the course of establishing a cult of reason and humanity. In the former Soviet Union clergy of all religions constituted one of the categories of 'former persons' who were denied civil standing in the Declaration of Rights that was promulgated in January 1918, and in the decades that followed hundreds of thousands of them and their family members were executed or died in camps in the campaign for 'scientific atheism'. In Mao's China countless temples were ravaged and an entire civilization almost destroyed in Tibet. In Chapter 4, I discuss the record of modern political religions in greater detail.

Throughout much of the twentieth century, terrible violence was inflicted in the service of secular faiths. In contrast, the organized atheism of the present century is mostly a media phenomenon and best appreciated as a type of entertainment.

2

Secular Humanism, a Sacred Relic

For its followers the religion of humanity seems different from the religions of the past. Having repudiated monotheism, they imagine they stand outside the view of the world that monotheism expressed. But while they may have rejected monotheist beliefs, they have not shaken off a monotheistic way of thinking. The belief that humans are gradually improving is the central article of faith of modern humanism. When wrenched from monotheistic religion, however, it is not so much false as meaningless.

For the ancient Greeks and Romans, history revealed no pattern other than the regular growth and decline of civilization – a rhythm not essentially different from those found in the natural world. There was no prospect of indefinite improvement. Judged by the standards of the time, civilization might improve for a while. But eventually the process would stall, then go into reverse. Rooted in the innate defects of the human animal, cycles of this kind could not be overcome. If the gods intervened, the result was only to make the human world even more unpredictable and treacherous.

Some ancient historians eliminated divine intervention in their accounts of events. Writing in the fifth century BC, the Greek historian Herodotus has the gods acting to punish wrongdoing (such as violation of temples), but there is no suggestion that they were interested in shaping the course of history. Herodotus' successor Thucydides wrote history without recourse to any kind of divine intervention. His *History of the Peloponnesian War* records a succession of mishaps in which human will and reason are confounded by archetypal human flaws. Thucydides has been called the father of 'scientific history'. But for him there were no laws of history, only the fact of recurring human folly.

A cyclical view of history was revived in Europe during the Renaissance by Niccolò Machiavelli. Rather than contesting Christian belief, the Florentine historian and adviser to princes stepped outside Christian ways of thinking. History was not a moral tale in which evil is punished or redeemed. A prince had to be ready to commit crime in order to protect the state. In order for virtue to survive, a ruler had to practise vice. Human goodness showed no tendency to increase over time. This view proved too uncomfortable to be adopted by Machiavelli's contemporaries, and it is one most secular thinkers have found intolerable.

Until the rise of Christianity, a cyclical view of history was taken for granted by practically everyone. When in eighteenth-century Europe religion began to be replaced by secular creeds, the Christian myth of history as a redemptive drama was not abandoned but renewed in another guise. A story of redemption through divine providence was replaced by one of progress through the collective efforts of humanity. Nothing like this could have developed from polytheistic religions, which take for granted that human beings will always have disparate goals and values.

PROGRESS, A CHRISTIAN MYTH

The modern faith in progress began with shifts in Christian thinking. Declaring itself superior to anything in the pagan or Jewish world, Christianity affirmed that a new order of things was open to everybody. Throughout much of Christian history it was believed that this transformation would occur when Jesus returned and founded the kingdom of God. After an earth-shaking battle with the dark forces that rule the world, evil would be destroyed and a new world would come into being. This apocalyptic myth fuelled the millenarian movements of medieval times – mass uprisings against Church and state inspired by the belief that history was about to end through an act of divine intervention.[1]

With the Reformation and the rise of 'post-millennialism' in seventeenth-century Protestantism, this myth gave way to one that was more human-centred. The belief that evil would be destroyed in an apocalyptic end-time was supplanted by the conviction that evil could be slowly diminished in history. Jesus would still return and rule over the world, but only after it had been transformed by human effort. Emptied of its transcendental content, this Christian myth is the source of modern meliorism – the idea that human life can be gradually improved. Unlike the dominant view of history in the ancient world, which recognized improvement but accepted that what had been gained would over time be lost, the modern neo-Christian belief in progress asserts that human life can be made better cumulatively and permanently.

Another element was important in the formation of this secular faith. Gnosticism entered into the religion of humanity via the belief that salvation was achieved by acquiring a special kind of knowledge. In the classical philosophies of the ancient world this knowledge was a type of mystical insight acquired through the practice of contemplation. In modern times it was knowledge gained through science. In each case it was believed that knowledge could bring deliverance from evil.

The modern myth of progress came into being as a fusion of Christian faith with Gnostic thinking. In Chapter 4, I will consider how Gnosticism shaped modern political religions – including liberalism. Here it is worth noting that while modern meliorism claims to be based in science, the idea that civilization improves throughout history has never been a falsifiable hypothesis. If it had been it would have been abandoned long ago.

For those who believe in progress, any regression that may occur can only be a temporary halt in an onward march to a better world. Yet if you look at the historical record without modern prejudices you will find it hard to detect any continuing strand of improvement. The triumph of Christianity brought with it the near-destruction of classical civilization. Libraries and museums, temples and statues were demolished or defaced on a vast scale in what has been described as 'the largest destruction of art the world has ever seen'.[2] Everyday life was hemmed in with unprecedented repression. While there was nothing in the pagan world of the liberal concern for individual free-dom, pluralism in ways of life was accepted as a matter of course. Since religion was not a matter of belief, no one was persecuted for heresy. Sexuality was not demonized as it would be in the Christian world, nor gay people stigmatized. While they were subordinate to men, women were freer than they would be once Christianity had triumphed.

Today everyone is sure that civilization has improved with mod-ern times. As we are forever being reminded, the medieval and early modern world was wracked by wars of religion. But faith-based vio-lence did not fade away with the arrival of the modern age. From the French Revolution onwards, Europe and much of the world were caught up in revolutions and wars fuelled by secular creeds such as Jacobinism and communism, Nazism and fascism and a belligerently evangelical type of liberalism. In the twenty-first century a potent source of faith-based violence has emerged in Islamist movements, which blend ideas borrowed from Leninism and fascism with fund-amentalist currents from within Islam.

It is true that slavery and torture were flaws of pre-modern soci-eties. But these practices have not disappeared. Slavery was reintroduced in the twentieth century on a vast scale in Nazi Ger-many and the Soviet and Maoist gulags. Slave auctions in the so-called Caliphate established by the Islamic State in parts of Iraq and Syria were advertised on Facebook. Human trafficking flour-ishes throughout much of the world. Torture has been renormalized. Banned in England in the mid-seventeenth century and in Europe by the Habsburg empress Maria Theresa in the late eighteenth, the practice was revived by the world's pre-eminent democracy when George W. Bush sanctioned it in the run-up to the invasion of Iraq.

Instead of being left behind, old evils return under new names. No thread of progress in civilization is woven into the fabric of his-tory. The cumulative increase of knowledge in science has no parallel in ethics or politics, philosophy or the arts. Knowledge increases at an accelerating rate, but human beings are no more reasonable than they have ever been. Gains in civilization occur from time to time, but they are lost after a few generations.

A commonplace in the ancient world, this fact is impossible for secular humanists to accept, or in many cases comprehend. They realize that the progress of civilization is not inevitable and no sort of perfection achievable. Humanity advances inch by inch, they say; the march to a better world will be long and hard. What these secular believers cannot digest is the fact that gains in ethics and politics regularly come and go – a fact that confounds any story of continuing human advance.

When secular thinkers tell the history of humankind as a story of progress they flatter themselves that they embody the progress of which they speak. At the same time they confirm that their view of the world has been inherited from monotheism. It was only with the invention of Christianity that a history of humankind began to be told. Before that point, there was no universal history. Many stories were told – the story of the Jewish people, the Greeks, the Romans and multitudes of others.

Modern thinkers say that telling history as a story of all humankind marks an advance. But along with Christian universalism came a militant intolerance – a trait that Christianity transmitted to its secular successors. For neo-Christian believers any way of life that fails or refuses to fit into a story of progress can be regarded as subhuman, exiled to the margins of history and then consigned to extinction.

Like the Christian monotheism from which it sprang, secular humanism is a garbled mix of Jewish religion and Greek philosophy. For Plato – the fountainhead of Gnosticism in western philosophy – the world of passing time is a veil that conceals a changeless spiritual reality. The Bible suggests a different view. In the Old Testament, contingency – the arbitrary fact that things happen as they do – is an ultimate reality. God created the world, and intervenes in it as he pleases.

These views of the world support diverging conceptions of human salvation. For those who follow Plato, humans are exiles from eternity; freedom consists in ascending from the realm of shadows and leaving behind the illusion of being a separate, time-bound individual. In biblical accounts, salvation is not an escape from contingency but a miraculous event in the contingent world. It was some such event that Jesus expected when he announced the kingdom of God.

Those who were saved would not be assimilated into an eternal spirit but would be brought back from the grave as corporeal human beings.

These Jewish and Greek views of the world are not just divergent but irreconcilably opposed. Yet from its beginnings Christianity has been an attempt to join Athens with Jerusalem. Augustine's Christian Platonism was only the first of many such attempts. Without knowing what they are doing, secular thinkers have continued this vain effort.

PLATO FOR THE MASSES

The formative impact of Plato's philosophy on the Christian religion can be seen in Augustine's debts to Plotinus. Reading the third-century mystic in Latin, Augustine absorbed an understanding of the human relationship with God that would shape Christianity and later the modern western idea of humanity.

For Plotinus, God is being itself, undifferentiated and timeless, while the things of this world are ephemeral and insubstantial. Humans are estranged from an absolute oneness, which alone is truly real. Salvation consists in reidentifying oneself with this Absolute, which Plotinus – borrowing the term from Stoic philosophy – called *Logos*, a cosmic principle of reason. Nothing in passing time is truly itself. Humans become what they really are only by merging with the eternal *Logos*. Until they reach that point, they are alienated from their nature.

In this vision salvation is not an event in time but the act of exiting from time. All that has made human beings what they have been – their memories, emotions and relationships – must be left behind as counting for nothing. There is no suggestion here that humankind can find redemption in history. Human conflicts are not staging-points in a march to some higher state but recurring clashes of ignorant armies in the night.

There is no place for progress in this view of things. But Platonistic philosophy came to be intermixed, first in Augustine and then in other Christian thinkers, with the belief that human salvation was achieved through an historical process of divine self-realization. The link between the two was a theogony – an account of how God comes into being – in which God could achieve full self-awareness only by creating a multitude of souls and joining in their struggles. Instead of contemplating its own perfection in a timeless realm, the *Logos* was revealing itself in history.

This fancy was first formulated explicitly by the ninth-century neo-Platonic mystic and Christian theologian John Scotus Erigena (c. 815–77). The philosophy of Plotinus contained an unanswerable question. If the Absolute is self-sufficient, why did the shadow-world in which humans pass their lives come into being? Erigena's response was that the Absolute needed to manifest itself in time in order to become fully self-aware. In the language of Christian theology, God created human souls so that God could know himself in them. Instead of being a stain on the face of eternity, humankind was a mirror in which Spirit could see itself. Shattering himself into infinitesimal fragments, God created the human world. History is the process in which these fragments are reassembled.

This account of God's return to himself became one of the sources of the modern belief that history is the story of the progress of humankind. Flowing through German religion, Erigena's vision moulded German philosophy. Transmitted through Christian mystics such as Angelus Silesius and Jakob Böhme, the notion that God created humankind in order to become more fully aware of his own nature morphed into G. W. F. Hegel's philosophy of the world-spirit and Karl Marx's humanism. Hegel imagined that he had synthesized all of human thought, whereas Marx believed that the human species would become properly aware of itself only in a future state of communism. But, for both of them, history was the process whereby humanity becomes a fully conscious agent. A self-realizing God was replaced by a self-deifying humanity.

A point of transition occurred when in his book *The Essence of Christianity* (1841) the radical philosopher Ludwig Feuerbach reversed the traditional relationship between God and humankind. Hegel had represented history as the unfolding of the world-spirit. Turning this theocentric view on its head, Feuerbach held that the world-spirit was an image of human possibilities projected into the heavens. It was not God but humankind that made history – an assertion Marx repeated and endorsed in his *Theses on Feuerbach* (1845).

Modern philosophies in which history is a process of human self-realization are therefore spin-offs from the mystical speculations of medieval theologians. When Hegel envisioned history as a rational process, he was able to do so because – like Plato and Plotinus – he believed the world was a manifestation of *Logos*.

The belief that humanity makes history in order to realize its full possibilities is a relic of mysticism. Unless you believe the species to be an instrument of some higher power, 'humanity' cannot do *anything*. What actually exists is a host of human beings with common needs and abilities but differing goals and values. If you set metaphysics aside, you are left with the human animal and its many contending ways of life.

Marx's view of history owes more to Platonic philosophy than Jewish messianic religion. In his once-celebrated *History of Western Philosophy* Bertrand Russell wrote:

> To understand Marx psychologically, one should use the following dictionary:
>
> Yahweh = Dialectical Materialism
>
> The Messiah = Marx
>
> The Elect = The Proletariat
>
> The Church = The Communist Party
>
> The Second Coming = The Revolution
>
> Hell = Punishment of the Capitalists
>
> The Millennium = The Communist Commonwealth
>
> The terms on the left give the emotional content of the terms on the right, and it is this emotional content, familiar to those who have had a Christian or Jewish upbringing, that makes Marx's eschatology credible.[3]

Russell's analysis leaves something to be desired. He assumed that Marx was the author of the system of ideas that came to be known as Marxism, which included theories such as dialectical materialism. In fact Marx never produced anything like an intellectual system. A nineteenth-century thinker responding to the events of his time, he voiced a succession of views that fail to cohere with each other or with what later came to be known as Marxism. The circumstances of his life as an émigré moving from country to country, always in need of money, precluded the long periods of continuous intellectual labour that are required for system-building. Even his greatest works – such as the monumental *Capital* – were left unfinished.

Marx's political views changed greatly during his lifetime. At points in the 1840s, they had something in common with those of twentieth-century anti-communists – not only was communism impractical in his view, he believed it was also undesirable. In 1842, he wrote that as a result of the spread of communist ideas 'our once blossoming commercial cities are no longer flourishing', while in 1848 he rejected the idea of revolutionary dictatorship as 'nonsense'. As a result of the influence of Engels, Marx has been seen as an admirer of Darwin. In fact Marx disliked Darwin's theory of natural selection because it left human progress 'purely accidental'. He preferred the work of the forgotten French ethnographer Pierre Trémaux, who argued that 'racial differences' have 'a natural basis' in biology – a common view at the time.

Marx endorsed many of the prevailing racial stereotypes. In his essay on *The Jewish Question* (1843–4), he equated Judaism with usury and (following Voltaire) condemned Jewish religion as a 'polytheism of many needs'.[4] Describing the German-Jewish socialist leader Ferdinand Lassalle, Marx wrote:

> It is now completely clear to me that, as proven by the shape of his head and the growth of his hair, he [Lassalle] stems from the Negroes who joined the march of Moses out of Egypt (if his mother or grandmother did not mate with a nigger). Now this combination of Jewry and Germanism with the negroid basic substance must bring forth a peculiar product. The pushiness of the lad is also nigger-like.[5]

Marx's shifting views reflected the prejudices of his time while being closely related to the political struggles in which he was involved. He was no more the founder of Marxism than Jesus was of Christianity. If anyone created Marxism, it was Engels – not only Marx's closest collaborator but also for many years the source of much of his income. Marx's financial dependency on his benefactor precluded open discussion of the many areas in which the two disagreed.

Neither the uncertain conditions of his life nor his own restless intelligence allowed Marx to fashion a system of ideas such as the one that bears his name. But Marx did have a view of history that he pursued throughout many of his writings, and Russell was right in thinking that an eschatological myth was at the heart of this view. But it was a myth inherited more from Christian Platonism than from Jewish religion. When Marx tells the story of human self-realization it leads back not to Jesus but to Paul and Augustine. Marx's philosophy of history is Christian theodicy repackaged as humanist myth.

In Marx's mythology the original Absolute is primitive communism – an imaginary condition in prehistory when humans lived without conflicts or divisions. History is the movement towards self-awareness of a species alienated from itself. When communism is realized at the end of history the species returns to its original unity with full self-consciousness.

In *Beyond Good and Evil*, Nietzsche described Christianity as 'Platonism for the masses' – an accusation that applies with equal or greater force to secular humanism. The faith that history has a built-in logic impelling humanity to a higher level is Platonism framed in historical terms. Marxists have thought of human development as being driven by new technologies and class conflict, whereas liberals have seen the growth of knowledge as the principal driver. No doubt these forces help shape the flow of events. But unless you posit a divinely ordained end-state there is no reason to think history has any overarching logic or goal.

For Plato and Plotinus, history was a nightmare from which the individual mind struggled to awake. Following Paul and Augustine, the Christian Erigena made history the emerging embodiment of *Logos*. With their unending chatter about progress, secular humanists project this mystical dream into the chaos of the human world.

JOHN STUART MILL, THE SAINT OF RATIONALISM

As we know it today it was John Stuart Mill (1806–73) who founded liberal humanism. Described by the piously Christian prime minister

W. E. Gladstone as 'the saint of rationalism', Mill spent a night in gaol for distributing pamphlets to working-class women detailing techniques of contraception and enjoyed a long, unconventional and by all accounts mutually fulfilling relationship with the feminist writer Harriet Taylor, whom he married on her husband's death. He served as a Member of Parliament for several years and authored studies of logic and economics that were used as textbooks for generations. He was also an avid botanist, a devotee of Romantic poetry and godfather of Bertrand Russell.

Raised by his Scottish father James Mill, a disciple of Jeremy Bentham, John Stuart Mill never agonized over Christian belief. In early adulthood, though, he did suffer a crisis of faith. The faith he struggled with was Utilitarianism, a version of secular humanism in which the goal of human action was the maximal satisfaction of wants – sometimes summarized as 'the greatest happiness of the greatest number' – which would be achieved by applying a process of calculation that Bentham described as a 'hedonistic calculus' or 'moral arithmetic'.

As he entered manhood, Mill was seized by a paralysing doubt regarding this Utilitarian creed. He wrote in his *Autobiography*: 'I was brought up from the first without any religious belief, in the ordinary acceptation of the term . . . I am thus one of the very few examples, in this country, of one who has, not thrown off religious belief, but never had it; I grew up in a negative state with regard to it.'[6] Mill thought of himself as an agnostic, but in having no use for an idea of God he was in truth an atheist.

At the same time Mill did have a faith – the conviction, shared by countless later believers in the religion of humanity, that the species could raise itself to a higher level of civilization through the exercise of reason. Where Mill differed from other secular believers in his or our own time was in not taking this faith for granted. Nowadays there are millions of liberal humanists who have never had a religion of the ordinary kind. Few of them have asked themselves – as Mill did – whether their faith in human improvement can be supported by reason.

Mill's account of what he describes as his 'mental crisis' is heartfelt:

I had what might truly be called an object in life: to be a reformer of the world ... This did very well for several years, during which the general improvement going on in the world and the idea of myself as engaged with others in struggling to promote it, seemed enough to fill up an interesting and animated existence. But the time came when I awakened from this as from a dream ... In this frame of mind it occurred to me to put the question directly to myself: 'Suppose that all your objects in life were realised; that all the changes in institutions and opinions that you are looking forward to, could be completely effected at this very instant; would this be a great joy and happiness to you?' And an irrepressible self-consciousness distinctly answered: 'No!' At this my heart sank within me; the whole foundation on which my life was constructed fell down. All my happiness was to have been found in the continual pursuit of this end. The end had ceased to charm, and how could there ever again be any interest in the means? I seemed to have nothing left to live for.

Mill's crisis had a comical side. He writes that one of the sources of pleasure he retained during this period was the enjoyment of music. But this satisfaction was 'much impaired' by the prospect that there might be a finite number of possible melodies:

I was seriously tormented by the thought of the exhaustibility of musical combinations. The octave consists only of five tones and two semi-tones, which can be put together in a limited number of ways, of which but a small proportion are beautiful: most of these, it seemed to me, must have already been discovered, and there could not be room for a long succession of Mozarts and Webers, to strike out, as these had done, entirely new and surpassingly rich veins of musical beauty.[7]

It is easy to dismiss this as a case of depression. Mill writes that he began to recover when he was reading the memoirs of the eighteenth-century French historian Jean-François Marmontel. A passage where the author describes his father's death came to Mill as 'a small ray of light': 'I was moved to tears. From this point my burthen grew lighter. The oppression of the thought that all feeling was dead within me, was gone. I was no longer hopeless ... Relieved from my ever present sense of irremediable wretchedness, I gradually found that the ordinary incidents of life could again give me some pleasure . . .'[8]

Plainly, Mill's crisis was bound up with his relationship with his father. His early education was an experiment in rationalism. Applying the theory that the human mind comes into the world as a blank slate, his father taught him Greek at the age of three and Latin when he was eight years old. This was done in the same room where his father himself worked. Mill passed his childhood in the company of a taskmaster who 'demanded of me not only the utmost I could do, but much that I could by no possibility have done'. During his training in Greek and Latin, he was 'forced to have recourse to him for every word which I did not know'.[9]

Mill spent the rest of his life reweaving his father's philosophy in light of the experiment to which he had been subjected as a child. The result was not a new system of ideas, he wrote, but 'no system: only a conviction that the true system was something much more complex and many-sided than I had previously any idea of'.[10] Mill never claimed to have formulated a unified view of the human world. Even so, he founded an orthodoxy – the belief in improvement that is the unthinking faith of people who think they have no religion.

As he noted, Mill was unusual in not having been reared in any traditional faith. But, like everyone else in mid-Victorian England, he was shaped in his thinking and feelings by Christianity. When he insisted that morality did not depend on religion, he invoked an idea of morality that was borrowed from Christian religion. When he affirmed that humankind was improving, he was relying on the belief that the human animal is a collective moral agent – an idea that also derives from Christianity. None of these assertions can be supported by empirical observation, supposedly the basis of Mill's philosophy.

Mill was aware that the religion of humanity could become an impediment to free thinking. From Comte – with whom he corresponded in French for many years – he imbibed the idea, discussed in the last chapter, that history progresses through a succession of stages, each more rational than the last. But what would become of the individuality he had discovered in himself as he emerged from his mental crisis? Comte's philosophy, Mill came to believe, led to the destruction of freedom. His *Essay on Liberty* (1859) was an attempt to fend off this prospect. The subject of innumerable philosophical controversies,[11] Mill's essay was criticized most incisively by the Russian radical writer and journalist Alexander Herzen, who read *On Liberty* soon after it was published, when he was living in London as an exile from Tsarism.

In Herzen's view, most human beings did not greatly value their individuality, if indeed they had any. They preferred a settled way of life and what Mill called 'the deep slumber of a decided opinion'. Why should those who sleepwalk through this way of life break away from it? As Herzen perceived, Mill had no answer:

> On what principle are we to awake the sleeper? In the name of what shall the flabby personality, magnetised by trifles, be inspired, be made discontented with its present way of life of railways, telegraphs, newspapers and cheap goods?
>
> Individuals do not step out of the ranks because there is not the occasion. For whom, for what, or against whom are they to come forward? The absence of energetic men is not a cause but a consequence.[12]

Mill did not explain why people should give up a safe life of conformity to become free-thinking individuals. In his essay on *Utilitarianism* he asserted, 'It is better to be a human being dissatisfied than a pig satisfied.'[13] If the pig thinks otherwise, it is because the pig does not know the pleasures of the life of the mind. Unlike Bentham, Mill wanted to make a qualitative distinction between higher and lower pleasures. Moral and intellectual pleasures were higher, those of the body lower. He had no doubt that the former were more satisfying than the latter.

Mill's certainty on this point is droll. A high-minded Victorian, he had too little acquaintance with the lower pleasures to make a considered judgement. He thought of himself as an empiricist for whom every belief must be tested at the bar of human experience. He forgot to apply this test to his own judgements of value. In *On Liberty*, he wrote, 'I regard utility as the ultimate appeal on all ethical questions,' then continued, 'but it must be utility in the largest sense, grounded on the permanent interests of man as a progressive being.'[14]

It seemed obvious to Mill that humankind is progressing. But that is far from being a self-evident truth. Certainly human beings have transformed their ways of living and the planet around them. It is less clear that they have improved themselves or the world they inhabit. In what sense is a Nazi, a communist or an Islamist an improvement on an ancient Epicurean, Stoic or Taoist? How are the murderous political creeds of modern times better than the traditional faiths of the past? These are questions Mill's latter-day disciples do not ask, still less answer.

According to Mill's official philosophy, everything we recognize in the world – physical objects, human beings – is constructed from sensory impressions. Sensations are the building-blocks of the world. Here Mill differs from the French materialists, such as La Mettrie, discussed earlier, who thought the building-blocks of the world were physical things. But if matter is an abstract concept that can be useful because it helps us deal with the world around us, what is 'humanity'? Mill's conception of the species was not based on observation. It reflected his moral beliefs, which were derived from Christianity. The evidence that the human animal learns from its mistakes and follies is at best mixed. On this point, empiricism and liberalism are at odds.

For all his secular upbringing, Mill never shook off the influence of Victorian Christian values. 'The authentic sayings of Jesus', he wrote in his essay on *The Utility of Religion*, 'are surely in harmony with the intellect and feelings of every good man and woman.'[15] Not having the benefits of later textual discoveries, Mill could not in fact know which if any of the recorded sayings of Jesus was authentic. In any case his claim that a Christian morality accorded with 'the intellect and feelings of every good man and woman' was contradicted in his own experience. He never doubted that Auguste Comte was a good man. But Comte lacked any sense of the value of freedom, which for Mill was central to the good life. Even among those Mill regarded as virtuous, there were deeper divergences in values than he admitted.

Above all, Mill never questioned the Christian idea that 'morality' is an overriding imperative. As a result, he failed to explain why anyone should want to be moral. He believed any rational person would want to promote collective well-being rather than their own self-interest. But if self-interest and the general welfare are at odds, why opt for self-sacrifice? Why do your utilitarian duty rather than what you want to do?

These questions were posed by the philosopher Henry Sidgwick (1838–1900), one of the greatest nineteenth-century minds. Like Mill, Sidgwick was a conscientious Victorian. Unlike Mill, he had been reared as a Christian. He remained so until he found he could not accept some of the Thirty-Nine Articles of the Anglican Church. In 1869 he resigned his Cambridge fellowship, which required assent to all of them.

Sidgwick identified fundamental difficulties in Utilitarian ethics. Mill believed there was only one ultimate principle governing practical life – the principle of utility, which says that what matters is maximizing pleasure or the satisfaction of desires (there are many versions of what 'utility' might mean) for everybody. Sidgwick identified two such principles, and found that reason could not decide between them.

In his book *Methods of Ethics*, first published in 1874, Sidgwick uncovered what he called 'the dualism of practical reason'. Rather than a single principle of utility, he concluded there were two principles governing practical life – self-interest and concern for the general welfare. Contrary to Mill, who struggled to show that general welfare should take priority, Sidgwick was clear that there is no rational basis for such a hierarchy.

Self-interest, Sidgwick pointed out, is not self-evidently rational. Unless we invoke a religious idea of the soul, human personality is no more than a succession of continuities in memory and behaviour. In that case, why should anyone favour their future self over their present self? The fundamental conflict in ethics was not the conflict between self-interest and general welfare but that between general welfare and the desires of the moment. Faced with these rival imperatives, reason was powerless. As Sidgwick put it at the end of *Methods of Ethics*, there was 'an ultimate and fundamental contradiction in our apparent intuitions of what is reasonable in conduct'.[16]

This was something he could not endure. He had already lost his Christian faith. The prospect of a universe lacking any 'moral government' was too much for him. He spent the rest of his life looking to science for a way out of the world that science – Darwinian biology in particular – had revealed. The science to which he turned was psychical research – an inquiry into paranormal phenomena that attracted many leading minds in late Victorian and Edwardian times, including the co-discoverer of natural selection, Alfred Russel Wallace.

Sidgwick lived in the hope that science would supply proof that the human mind survived bodily death. Why he believed this would fill the hole he had found in ethics is unclear. The mind might survive death only to find itself in another world that was just as chaotic. Rigorously honest in his investigations, Sidgwick died without finding any evidence for posthumous existence. In old age he told a close friend, 'As I look back on my life I see little but wasted hours.'

Even if he found the proof of the afterlife he was looking for, Sidgwick might not have been satisfied. Some years after his death a text purporting to come from him was produced by a medium. He had survived bodily death, 'Sidgwick' reported, to find himself in another world; but 'the Great Problem' was unsolved. The universe remained as mysterious as ever. Baffled in death as he had been in life, 'Sidgwick' concluded: 'We can no more solve the riddle of death by dying than we can solve the problem of living by being born.'[17]

BERTRAND RUSSELL, UNWILLING SCEPTIC

Mill was an empiricist, who held that all of our beliefs should be based on experience. Yet neither he nor the secular thinkers who followed him subjected their belief in progress to any empirical test. Mill's liberal posterity failed to square their empiricism with their faith in continuing improvement.

The case of Mill's godson Bertrand Russell, whose views on Marx's philosophy of history were considered in the last chapter, is instructive. Born in 1872 into an aristocratic liberal family – his grandfather Lord John Russell had brought in the Great Reform Act of 1832, which extended the franchise – he was like Mill in being educated at home. His father Lord Amberley was an atheist who left instructions in his will requiring that his son be brought up as an agnostic, but Russell's grandmother Countess Russell overturned the requirement in the courts and he was reared as a Christian. Having spent a solitary childhood during which he recorded his doubts regarding Christianity in a secret diary written in code, he abandoned Christian belief after reading Mill's *Autobiography* at the age of eighteen.

He continued to be preoccupied with religion. He had a number of mystical experiences in the course of his life. One occurred in 1901, when visiting the sickbed of the wife of his Cambridge colleague A. N. Whitehead:

> Suddenly the ground seemed to give way beneath me, and I found myself in quite another region. Within five minutes I went through some such reflections as the following: the loneliness of the human soul is unendurable; nothing can penetrate it except the highest intensity of the sort of love that religious teachers have preached; whatever does not spring from this motive is harmful, or at best useless; it follows that war is wrong, that a public school education is abominable, that the use of force is to be deprecated, and that in human relations one should penetrate to the core of loneliness in each person and speak to that . . . At the end of those five minutes I had become a completely different person. For a time, a sort of mystic illumination possessed me . . .[18]

Russell's work in logic, where he was a world-class pioneer, served a mystical impulse. For a time he seems to have believed that mathematical truths might exist in an eternal Platonic domain beyond time and the visible world. Until he was persuaded otherwise by George Santayana, he believed that values such as goodness and truth subsisted in the same ethereal realm. He spent much of his life searching for this heavenly domain and never found it.

Like the seventeenth-century Dutch-Jewish philosopher Benedict Spinoza, whose version of atheism will be examined in Chapter 7, Russell looked to mathematics for perfect knowledge of truth. He was fully aware that this was a religious quest. In 1912 he wrote a novella, *The Perplexities of John Forstice*, in which the protagonist reaches inner peace when he accepts that a saintly nun reveals a spiritual reality beyond the human world. In later life Russell found the story 'much too favourable to religion'. In his *Autobiography*, he wrote of a persisting need for something that transcended the human world:

> I have imagined myself in turn a Liberal, a Socialist, or a Pacifist, but I have never been any of these things, in any profound sense . . . What Spinoza calls 'the intellectual love of God' has seemed to me the best thing to live by, but I have not had even the somewhat abstract God that Spinoza allowed himself to whom to attach my intellectual love. I have loved a ghost, and in loving a ghost my inmost self has itself become spectral . . . The sea, the stars, the night wind in waste places, mean more to me than even the human beings I love best, and I am conscious that human affection is to me at bottom an attempt to escape from the vain search for God.[19]

In a footnote dated 1967, Russell writes that this 'is no longer true'. Marrying four times and having countless affairs, Russell finally found fulfilment with the American writer Edith Finch, whom he married in 1952. He died in 1970.

Russell spent much of his long life as a sceptic, and professed to be happy to live with doubt. Yet he had vast hopes of social transformation that a sceptical outlook could hardly justify. Submitting religion to the test of sceptical doubt, he found religion wanting. It seemed not to occur to him to apply the same scepticism to his high-minded hopes of improving the world. There is a telling contrast here with ancient Greek sceptics, who instead cultivated detachment from the world.

A 'scientific philosophy', Russell wrote in 1928, could fashion a 'new morality' that would 'turn our earth into a paradise'.[20] How this remarkable metamorphosis would come about he did not explain. He believed that reason did not move human beings to action. Only the passions could do that, and reason was their servant. But if reason cannot fix human ends, it certainly cannot remake the human world. All it can do is enable human beings to achieve their goals more effectively – whatever these goals may be. Sceptical in philosophy, Russell tended to be credulous in politics.

At times he faced realities that liberal opinion preferred to ignore. Written after he had visited Soviet Russia and met Lenin, his book *The Practice and Theory of Bolshevism* (1920) was one of the first to grasp that methodical mass killing was central to the Bolshevik project. 'A great part of the despotism which characterises the Bolsheviks', he writes, 'belongs to the essence of their social philosophy, and would have to be reproduced, even if in a milder form, wherever that philosophy became dominant.' Russell was clear that Bolshevism was a vehicle for religious needs: 'Bolshevism as a social phenomenon is to be reckoned as a religion, not as an ordinary political movement.'[21]

Russell's insight into the Bolshevik regime earned him the mistrust of the progressive intelligentsia for many years. He returned to the conventional political hopes of his day when he visited China, where he contracted pneumonia and was reported to have died, enabling him to read his own obituaries. The solution to China's difficulties, he opined in *The Problem of China* (1922), was 'international socialism'. Having been a pacifist during the First World War, when he was briefly imprisoned under the Defence of the Realm Act and stripped by his colleagues of his fellowship at Trinity College, Cambridge, he opposed British rearmament against the rising threat of Nazism. By 1940 he had come to accept the necessity for war. When the Soviet Union acquired nuclear weapons, he argued in favour of a pre-emptive nuclear strike that would enable the western powers to set up a world government. Later he would be a prominent supporter of unilateral nuclear disarmament.

Though the stances Russell adopted changed over the course of his long life, he never gave up the belief that human life could be transformed by the use of reason. He could not resolve the conflict between sceptical doubt and faith in progress. Except towards the end of his life, tranquillity of mind eluded him.

A subliminal awareness that his visions of social transformation might be deceptive may explain Russell's friendship with Joseph Conrad. Describing his first meeting with the novelist Russell wrote:

> we talked with continually increasing intimacy. We seemed to sink through layer after layer of what was superficial, till gradually both

reached the central fire. It was an experience unlike any other that I have known. We looked into each other's eyes, half appalled and half intoxicated to find ourselves in such a region. The emotion was as intense as passionate love, and at the same time all-embracing. I came away bewildered, and hardly able to find my way among ordinary affairs.[22]

Russell was drawn to Conrad, and with the writer's blessing named his son, the historian Conrad Russell, after him. Yet Russell could never bring himself to accept Conrad's scepticism regarding progress. Unlike Russell, Conrad – whose version of atheism will be discussed in Chapter 6 – found belief in human improvement as incredible as any religion.

FROM NIETZSCHE TO AYN RAND

Few thinkers were more different than Henry Sidgwick and Friedrich Nietzsche. Sidgwick was unfailingly conscientious in his pursuit of truth, Nietzsche an intellectual adventurer who came to doubt the value of truth. Yet the two converged on a vital point. Once theism is left behind, not only much of religious morality but 'morality' itself must come into question. Here Sidgwick was more radical than Mill and more sceptical than Russell.

Following Christian precedent, Sidgwick believed that morality consisted of universal laws or principles.[23] This is not how ethics was understood by the polytheistic Greeks, who had no conception of 'morality' as we nowadays understand it. They understood ethics as the whole art of life, which included beauty and pleasure as values no less important than those that Christian and post-Christian cultures consider peculiarly 'moral'.

It is not only the assertion that 'moral' values must take precedence over all others that has been inherited from Christianity. So has the belief that all human beings must live by the same morality. This is not the same as saying 'If God is dead, all things are permitted,' as Nietzsche is supposed to have done. (The saying actually comes from a character in Dostoevsky's novel *The Brothers Karamazov*, which I will discuss in Chapter 5.) Human beings develop moralities as a normal part of living with each other, but no single morality is uniquely human. Understood as a set of categorical principles binding on all human beings, 'morality' itself is one more relic of monotheism – possibly the most important of them all.

If they are philosophers, secular thinkers will tell you that Nietzsche was guilty of a 'genetic fallacy' – the error of thinking that beliefs that have depended on falsehoods must themselves be false. Just because the idea of a universal moral law originated in religion, these philosophers say, does not mean the idea must be abandoned once religion has been rejected. Wheeling in the rusty old apparatus of the genetic fallacy hardly settles the question, however. Without a law-giver, what can a universal moral law mean? If you think of morality as part of the natural behaviour of the human animal, you find that humans do not live according to a single moral code. Unless you think one of them has been mandated by God, you must accept the variety of moralities as a part of what it means to be human.

At this point the spectre of relativism is sure to appear on the scene – as it did in the last chapter, when it was suggested that science need not eventuate in one true view of the world. If there are many moralities, it will be asked, how can there be truth in ethics? Well, if you leave theism behind you must accept that human values cannot be independent of human needs and decisions. Some values may be humanly universal – being tortured or persecuted is bad for all human beings, for example. But universal values do not make a *universal morality*, for these values often conflict with each other. Do you want more liberty at the price of less security? Peace if it means continuing injustice? When individuals and groups choose between conflicting universal values, they create different moralities. Anyone who wants their morality secured by something beyond the fickle human world had better join an old-fashioned religion.

In France, where atheists are better educated than in English-speaking countries, Nietzsche continues to be central to the discussion of religion. Thinkers like Georges Bataille have explored the prospects of a 'difficult atheism' that does not take any set of values for granted. Today the popular French philosopher Michel Onfray acknowledges Nietzsche's pivotal role in modern atheism, writing that 'Nietzsche introduced transvaluation: atheism is not an end in itself. Do away with God, but then what? Another morality, a new ethic, values never before thought of because unthinkable, this innovation is what makes it possible to arrive at atheism and to surpass it. A formidable task, and one still to be brought to fruition.'[24] Not much has come of these new atheisms. Bataille's 'atheology' produced nothing coherent, while Onfray's new ethics turns out to be a reheated version of Bentham's Utilitarianism. But at least these French thinkers recognize there is a problem about atheist values, and do not simply regurgitate some secular version of Christian morality.

Given that he is one of the most widely read atheist writers of all time, Nietzsche's absence from English-speaking atheist discourse is an interesting omission. He is not neglected because he was a forerunner of fascism. Nietzsche attacked nationalism, mocked the Prussian state and ridiculed the faux-Darwinism that was emerging as the dominant German ideology. He preferred the religion of the Old Testament to that of the New and loathed the anti-Semites who were so prominent at the time – including his repulsive sister Elisabeth Förster-Nietzsche, who married an anti-Semitic high-school teacher with whom she travelled to Paraguay to set up an 'Aryan colony', one of many services to racism that Hitler cited when he attended her funeral. But if Nietzsche was not a fascist or a proto-Nazi, neither was he any kind of liberal. This may be why he is screened out from so much of current atheist thinking.

An atheist *because* he rejected liberal values, Nietzsche is the ghost at the liberal humanist feast. In *The Anti-Christ*, he condemned the Christian religion in the strongest terms: 'In Christianity the instincts of the subjugated and oppressed come into the foreground: it is the lowest classes which seek their salvation in it.'[25] In suggesting that Christianity began as a 'slave-religion' Nietzsche was on shaky ground. His account of Christian origins is not very different from the standard Christian story, which has Jesus attracting his disciples from among the poor and outcast. He underestimates the gulf between the teachings of Jesus and the religion founded by Paul. Writing of Paul as 'quintessentially Jewish',[26] he passes over how Paul severed the Jewish roots of Jesus' teaching by turning it into a universal creed.

While Nietzsche may be a compelling critic of Christian values, he never succeeded in shaking off these values himself. The son of a Lutheran pastor, he led an ascetic existence. There was always an aura of otherworldliness around him. He renounced a brilliant academic career for the life of a wandering scholar. When he lived in a modest guest house in Genoa in the early 1880s, his fellow guests called him *il piccolo santo* – the little saint. While visiting Turin in 1889 he broke down after seeing a horse being beaten in the street, and proceeded to fire off letters to friends and various European dignitaries, signing them as 'Dionysus' or 'the Crucified'. The causes of his madness are disputed, with some explaining it as a side-effect of syphilis, which he may have contracted as a student. Until he died in 1900 he was under the care of his sister, who bowdlerized his thought in books (notably the posthumously published *Will to Power*) that she and others composed from passages they cobbled together from his notes.

An implacable enemy of Christianity, Nietzsche was also an incurably Christian thinker. Like the Christians he despised, he regarded the human animal as a species in need of redemption. Without God, humankind faced 'nihilism' – life without meaning. But nihilism could be avoided if humans willed into being the meaning God had once secured. Only a few would ever be capable of this feat. It was these exceptional individuals – the supermen lauded in *Thus Spake Zarathustra* – who would redeem humanity from a senseless existence. Nietzsche's *Übermensch* or superman played a Christ-like role.

Nietzsche's thought continues to be a formative influence. It has been particularly important when its influence is denied. An example can be found in the work of one of the last century's most influential atheist writers, Ayn Rand.

Fastidious philosophers will sniff at including Rand in a list of atheist thinkers. Yet she is one of the most popular atheist writers, and the only one who has had an impact on contemporary politics. Condemning his philosophy as a betrayal of reason, Rand disavowed Nietzsche entirely. But there can be no doubt that a version of his ideas shaped her way of thinking.

Born in Russia in 1905, Rand left the Soviet Union at the age of twenty. Her first published novel, *We the Living* (1936), a fictionalized account of her experiences in the early Soviet period, contains a number of clues about the origins of her later philosophy. The heroine of the novel, Kira Argounova, also tries to leave the Soviet Union but fails and dies in the attempt. Kira has a Bolshevik lover, whom she admires not for his values and goals but for the ruthlessness with which he pursues them. Several passages in the first print of the book, which attested to this admiration, were excised by Rand from later editions.

In a foreword to the American edition that appeared in 1959, Rand told the reader that in some places she 'reworded the sentences and clarified their meaning, without changing their content . . . The novel remains what and as it was.'[27] Rand's insistence that nothing of importance had been changed was disingenuous. She had made some crucial revisions. As a result, the first edition has become a rare book that can cost tens of thousands of dollars to buy.

Consulting a first edition, I found the following exchange between Kira and her communist lover Victor. Kira tells Victor – who 'looked like a tenor in an Italian grand opera . . . the broad shoulders, the flaming black eyes, the wavy, unruly black hair, the flashing smile, the healthy arrogant assurance of every movement' – why she admires his ruthlessness:

> I loathe your ideals. I admire your methods. If one believes one is right, one shouldn't wait to convince millions of fools, one might just as well force them . . . What *are* your masses but mud to be ground under foot, fuel to be burned for those who deserve it? What is the people but millions of puny, shrivelled, helpless souls, that have no thoughts of their own, no dreams of their own, no will of their own, who eat and sleep and chew helplessly the words put into their mildewed brains.[28]

Here – and, in a less overt form, throughout Rand's writings – a violent rejection of the sacrificial ethics of Christianity is combined with a willingness to sacrifice countless human lives for the sake of a few self-styled superior individuals.

Much that seems strange in Rand's life and writings becomes clearer once Nietzsche's ideas – a vulgarized version of them, at any rate – are taken into account. The admiration she expressed in her journal in 1928 for William Hickman is telling in this regard. An armed robber and kidnapper who murdered and dismembered a twelve-year-old girl he had abducted for ransom, Hickman might seem an unlikely candidate for the title of *Übermensch*. Yet Rand quoted with approval a dictum attributed to him – 'What is good for me is right' – commenting in her journal: 'The best and strongest expression of a real man's psychology I have heard.'[29]

Hickman's dictum is far from anything that can be derived from Nietzsche. As he dissected human values in *The Genealogy of Morality*, Nietzsche found them inherently conflicting. Good could come of evil, truth of falsehood. Some of the most precious achievements of civilization emerged from error and illusion. The ascetic Christian morality he loathed had given birth to a passion for truth that culminated in atheism. There is nothing of this subtlety in Rand.

Rand's views were not always as eccentric as they seem today. Practically every literate person in Russia from 1890 up to the revolutions of 1917 was exposed to some variant of Nietzsche's ideas.[30] There were Nietzschean Christians and Nietzschean pagans, Nietzschean Bolsheviks and Nietzschean Tsarists. Young people were particularly attuned to Nietzsche's ideas, which surfaced in the music of Alexander Scriabin and the writings of Maxim Gorky. When Rand was growing up in Russia, Nietzsche was ubiquitous as a cultural influence. It is hardly surprising that her attitudes should have reflected those that were popularly associated with him.

More interesting is the way Rand adapted her version of Nietzsche's ideas to American folk-mythology. Mixing them with borrowings from Aristotle and John Locke, she called the farrago that resulted 'Objectivism'. She produced a bible for the faithful in the 1,200 pages of *Atlas Shrugged*, first published in 1957, which has sold millions of copies.

In the book Nietzsche's *Übermensch*, represented in *We the Living* as a Bolshevik commissar, became a heroic American capitalist, John Galt. Forecasting the imminent destruction of the corrupted capitalism of his time, Galt offers other capitalists salvation in a hidden community, Galt's Gulch, an enclave in a Colorado mountain valley that will be preserved in the coming end-time. One fact about *Atlas Shrugged* that has gone unnoticed is that it is a reinvention of Christian apocalyptic myth. Here too Rand borrowed from Nietzsche.

In ethics Rand promoted an extreme version of rationalism according to which morality can be derived from principles of logic. To examine her arguments for this view would be tedious, since they are thoroughly silly. It is more useful to consider the ethical outlook she promoted. In Rand's work Nietzsche's defence of aristocratic individualism became an apology for laissez-faire capitalism. The *Übermensch* reappeared as an indignant businessman grumbling about taxes.

In Rand's ethics the worst vice is altruism. In *The Virtue of Self-ishness: a new concept of egoism* (1964), she rejected any conception of morality in which it is essentially concerned with the welfare of others. The only goal of any rational individual should be their own well-being. But Rand's conception of well-being was heavily moralized. It is not the welfare of any actually existing human being that counts, but that of an abstraction lacking in many human qualities. Actual human beings are only fitfully moved by anything that might be called rational self-interest. They need to sacrifice themselves, sometimes for the sake of others they care for and sometimes in the service of ideas that may have little or no meaning.

Rand's cult aimed to govern every aspect of life. She was a dedicated smoker, and her followers were instructed that they had to smoke as well. Not only did Rand smoke, she used a cigarette-holder – so that when she addressed large audience of the faithful, a thousand cigarette-holders would move in unison with hers.[31] It was not for nothing that the ultra-individualists who became Rand's disciples were described within the movement as 'the Collective'. The selection of marriage partners was also controlled. In her view of things, rational human beings should not associate with those that are irrational. There could be no worse example of this than two people joined together in marriage by mere emotion, so officers of the cult were empowered to pair Rand's disciples only with others who also subscribed to the faith. The marriage ceremony included pledging devotion to Rand, then opening *Atlas Shrugged* at random to read aloud a passage from the sacred text.[32]

Rand pronounced on a wide range of issues, including what was the best kind of dance. Only one type of dancing was truly rational. Some – like the tango – were low-level, semi-instinctual physical performances lacking any intellectual content. Others – the foxtrot, possibly – she rejected as being too cerebral. What then was the only dance that, combining mind and body, could be approved as being truly rational? Tap-dancing. Fred Astaire may not have known it, but he embodied the opposing forces of reason and instinct in an ideal synthesis. Tap-dancing was the cultural form that Nietzsche had been searching for in his first important work, *The Birth of Tragedy*: a fusion of Dionysian vitality with Apollonian harmony.

It might seem unlikely that a cult of this kind could exercise any public influence. But the maddest ideas are quite often the most influential, and Rand's cod-philosophy has had a discernible impact on American politics. Intermixed with Christian fundamentalism, it inspired the twenty-first-century Tea Party. One of the movement's leading lights, Senator Rand Paul – not named after Rand; his first name is 'Randall' – has boasted of being a 'big fan of Rand', though he is also a professed Catholic believer. Randian ideas have had an influence on American public policy. The ex-chairman of the Federal Reserve Bank Alan Greenspan was a former disciple of Rand, who – despite being anathematized by more orthodox believers for backtracking on the virtues of the gold standard – never entirely renounced the Objectivist faith. To his credit, Greenspan has suffered occasional spasms of doubt. In testimony to a Senate Committee in October 2008, following the financial crash, he admitted that his 'ideology' of the free market might be 'flawed' as an account of 'how the world works'.

For all its absurdities or because of them, Rand's version of atheism was one of the most widely disseminated in the second half of the twentieth century. But the chief significance of her ideas is not their popularity. It is in showing the protean character of atheism, which has inspired many varieties of ethics and politics.

Modern atheists can be individualists like Rand, socialists like Karl Marx, liberals like John Stuart Mill or fascists like Charles Maurras. They can revere altruism as the embodiment of all that is truly human with Auguste Comte, or revile altruists as thoroughly anti-human with Ayn Rand. Without exception, these atheists have been convinced they were promoting the cause of humanity. In every case, the species whose progress they believed they were advancing was a phantom of their imagination.

Ancient atheists were more dispassionate. The philosophy of the Epicureans – beautifully presented by Lucretius in his *De Rerum Natura* (*The Nature of Things*) – promoted an ethics in which gentle pleasures and peace of mind are the chief ends of human life. Epicureans aimed to insulate themselves from the sorrows of their fellow humans. The opening lines of Book Two of Lucretius' poem express the attitude of serene indifference to the mass of humankind they cultivated:

> A joy it is, when the strong winds of storm
> Sir up the waters of a mighty sea,
> To watch from the shore the troubles of another.
> No pleasure this in any man's distress,
> But joy to see the ills from which you are spared,
> And joy to see great armies locked in conflict
> Across the plains, yourself free from the danger.[33]

Watching calmly as others drowned in misery, the Epicureans were content in the tranquil retreat of their secluded gardens. 'Humanity' could do what it pleased. It was no concern of theirs.

3

A Strange Faith in Science

In 1929, the Thinker's Library, a series of books published by the Rationalist Press Association in London to counter the influence of religion in Britain, produced an English translation of the German biologist Ernst Haeckel's 1899 book *The Riddle of the Universe*. Selling half a million copies in Germany, the book was translated into dozens of other languages. Strongly hostile to Jewish and Christian traditions, Haeckel founded a new religion called Monism, which spread widely among intellectuals in central Europe. Among Monist tenets was a 'scientific anthropology' according to which the human species was composed of a hierarchy of racial groups, with white Europeans at the top.

At the time 'scientific racism' was not unusual in books promoting rationalism. The Thinker's Library also featured works by Julian Huxley, grandson of Thomas Henry Huxley, the Victorian biologist who became known as 'Darwin's bulldog' because of his vigorous defence of natural selection. Like Haeckel a proponent of a 'religion of science', Julian Huxley joined Haeckel in promoting theories of innate racial inequality. In 1931, he wrote that there was 'a certain amount of evidence that the Negro is an earlier product of human evolution than the Mongolian or the European, and as such might be expected to have advanced less, both in body and in mind'.

In the early twentieth century such attitudes were commonplace among rationalists. In his best-selling book *Anticipations* (1901) H. G. Wells, also a contributor to the Thinker's Library, wrote of a new world order ruled by a scientific elite drawn from the most advanced peoples of the world. Regarding the fate of 'backward' or 'inefficient' peoples, he wrote: 'And for the rest, those swarms of black and brown, and dirty-white, and yellow people, who do not come into the needs of efficiency? Well, the world is a world, not a charitable institution, and I take it that they will have to go . . . It is their portion to die out and disappear.'[1]

By the late 1930s these views were becoming suspect. In 1935, only a few years after writing of 'the Negro' as a less advanced product of human evolution, Huxley was writing that 'the concept of race is hardly definable in scientific terms'. There had been no major development in biology or anthropology in the years between these pronouncements. What altered Huxley's views was the rise of Nazism, which showed how racial theories could be applied in practice. After the Second World War Huxley did not pronounce on racial issues again, though he never renounced a belief in improving the quality of the human population through eugenics – a position he also shared with Haeckel.

Huxley's 'evolutionary humanism' asserted that if humankind was to ascend to a higher level, evolution would have to be consciously planned. Some religious thinkers followed Huxley in thinking in this way. A. N. Whitehead (1861–1947) and Samuel Alexander (1859–1938) developed a type of 'evolutionary theology' in which the universe was becoming more conscious of itself – a process that would culminate in the emergence of a Supreme Being much like the God of monotheistic religion. The French Jesuit theologian Pierre Teilhard de Chardin (1881–1955) developed a similar view in which the universe was evolving towards an 'Omega Point' of maximal consciousness.

All these philosophies rely on an idea of evolution. There is a problem, however. As understood in Darwin's theory, the universe is not in any sense evolving towards a higher level. Thinking of evolution as a movement towards greater consciousness misses Darwin's achievement, which was to expel teleology – explaining things in terms of the purposes they may serve rather than the causes that produced them – from science. As he wrote in his *Autobiography*, 'There seems to be no more design in the variability of organic beings, and in the action of natural selection, than in the course in which the wind blows.'[2]

As Darwin makes clear in this passage, natural selection is a purposeless process. He did not always stick with this view, however. On the last page of *On the Origin of Species*, he wrote:

> We may be certain that the ordinary succession by generations has never once been broken, and that no cataclysm has desolated the whole world. Hence we may look with some confidence to a future of great length. And as natural selection works solely for the good of each being, all corporeal and mental endowments will tend to progress to perfection.[3]

In fact the theory of natural selection contains no idea of progress or of perfection. Darwin's inability always to accept the logic of his own theory is revealing. An eminent Victorian, he could not help believing that natural selection favoured 'progress to perfection'. Many less scrupulous thinkers have followed Darwin in this belief. But not only is it at odds with Darwin's account of evolution as a non-directional process. If evolution had a direction, human beings need not accept it. What if the world was evolving towards new forms of slavery? In that case, it would be better to resist evolution than go along with it.

EVOLUTION VS ETHICS

The dangers of confusing evolution with ethics were recognized by Julian Huxley's grandfather. T. H. Huxley was concerned that Darwin's account of natural selection could be used to promote ideologies such as Victorian individualism. He was strongly opposed to what he called 'the gladiatorial theory of existence' – the misguided application of the idea of 'survival of the fittest' to social questions. In a lecture given in Oxford in 1893, three years before he died, Huxley observed:

> Cosmic evolution may teach us how the good and evil tendencies of man have come about: but, in itself, it is incompetent to furnish any better reason why what we call good is preferable to what we call evil than we had before ... The fanatical individualism of our time attempts to apply the analogy of cosmic nature to society ... The

cosmic process has no sort of relation to moral ends . . . Let us understand, once and for all, that the ethical progress of society depends,
not on imitating the cosmic process, still less in running away from it,
but in combating it.[4]

Equating evolution with progress is a misuse of Darwinism that pre-
dated Darwin's theory. The Victorian prophet of laissez-faire capitalism
Herbert Spencer identified the two in his book *Social Statics*, published
in 1851. It was Spencer who coined the expression 'survival of the fittest' in his book *Principles of Biology* (1864), written after he had read
Darwin's *Origin of Species* (1859). Later Darwin adopted the expression himself, though he never used it for political ends.

Despite Huxley's warnings, evolution and progress continue to be
confused. Bookshops are filled with volumes claiming to reveal the
evolution of morality. If Darwin's theory is true – and it is the best
account of how the human animal emerged to date – the moralities
human beings practise must have an evolutionary explanation. But
this says nothing about which morality anyone should adopt, or
whether they should be moral at all. As Huxley pointed out in his
lecture, morality and immorality are both of them products of evolution: 'The thief and the murderer follow nature just as much as the
philanthropist.'

Theories of social evolution mirror the intellectual fashions of the
time. If Herbert Spencer used evolutionary ideas to vindicate un-
trammelled capitalism, Haeckel and the early Julian Huxley used
these ideas to bolster belief in European racial superiority. Others
used them to prop up their political views. In a book co-authored
with her husband Sydney Webb, *Soviet Communism: a new civilization?*, first published in 1935, the sociologist Beatrice Webb – at one
time Herbert Spencer's assistant – suggested that Stalin's Russia
embodied the next stage of social evolution. (The question mark was
removed from later editions.) In a famous essay 'The End of History?' published in the American magazine *National Interest* in the
summer of 1989, Francis Fukuyama was in no doubt that an evolutionary process was at work leading to the advance of 'democratic
capitalism' throughout most of the world. Like the Webbs, Fukuyama later removed the question mark, which does not feature in his

book *The End of History and the Last Man* (1992). Neither the Webbs' nor Fukuyama's prognostications have been borne out by events.

Social evolution is an exceptionally bad idea. But bad ideas rarely evolve into better ones. Instead they mutate, and reproduce themselves in new guises.

RACISM AND ANTI-SEMITISM IN THE ENLIGHTENMENT

When Ernst Haeckel and Julian Huxley used science to bolster ideas of European racial superiority, they were taking a path cleared by earlier rationalist thinkers. Versions of racism have precedents in the writings of some of the leading philosophers of the Enlightenment.

Nowadays there is unending talk of 'Enlightenment values' in which human dignity and equality are assumed to be central. But if you look at the Enlightenment's most celebrated figures – David Hume, Immanuel Kant and Voltaire – you find that ideas of racial hierarchy are central to their thinking. Much of the Enlightenment was an attempt to demonstrate the superiority of one section of humankind – that of Europe and its colonial outposts – over all the rest.

Evangelists for the Enlightenment will say this was a departure from the 'true' Enlightenment, which is innocent of all evil. Just as religious believers will tell you that 'true' Christianity played no part in the Inquisition, secular humanists insist that the Enlightenment had no responsibility for the rise of modern racism. This is demonstrably false. Modern racist ideology is an Enlightenment project.

Consider David Hume. In a note attached to his essay on 'National Character', the Scottish sceptic wrote:

> I am apt to suspect the negroes, and in general all the other species of men (for there are four or five different kinds) to be naturally inferior to the whites. There never was a civilized nation of any other complexion than white, nor even any individual eminent in either action or speculation. No ingenious manufactures among them, no arts, no

sciences. On the other hand, the most rude and barbarous of the whites, such as the ancient Germans, the present Tartars, have still something eminent about them, in their valour, form of government, or some other particular. Such a uniform and constant difference could not happen in so many countries and ages, if nature had not made an original distinction betwixt these breeds of men. Not to mention in our colonies, there are negroes dispersed throughout all of Europe, of which none ever discovered any symptoms of ingenuity, tho' low people, without education, will start up amongst us, and distinguish themselves in every profession. In Jamaica indeed they talk of one negroe as a man of parts and learning; but 'tis likely he is admired on very slender accomplishments, like a parrot, who speaks a few words plainly.

Hume's claims were used by Kant – along with Hume, one of the two greatest philosophers of the Enlightenment – to suggest that 'the Negroes of Africa have by nature no feeling that arises over the trifling'. In his *Observations on the Beautiful and Sublime* Kant wrote:

Mr Hume challenges anyone to cite a simple example in which a Negro has shown talents, and asserts that among the hundreds of thousands of blacks who are transported elsewhere from their countries, although many of them have been set free, still not a single one was ever found who presented anything great in art or science or any other praiseworthy quality, even though among the whites some continually rise aloft from the lowest rabble, and through superior gifts earn respect from the world. So fundamental is the difference between these two races of men, and it appears to be as great as in regard to mental capacities as in colour.[5]

Here Hume and Kant were not far from saying that black people belong in some lesser anthropoid species. The idea that pre-human species linger on in the semblance of human beings was not new. Polygenetic accounts of human origins had been around at least since the discovery of the New World. The Renaissance philosopher Paracelsus wrote that indigenous American peoples were not descended from the biblical Adam but instead from a source that produced

nymphs and sirens – creatures without souls. A theological justifica-
tion for this view was attempted from the mid-sixteenth century
onwards in the pre-Adamite theory, which held that some human
beings were descended from a species that existed before Adam.

This was contrary to the biblical account in which all humans are
equal descendants of Adam and Eve, and for this reason the pre-
Adamite theory was rejected by many Christian thinkers. Among the
sharpest of these critics was Bartolomé de Las Casas, a contemporary of Christopher Columbus, former slave-owner and later Bishop
of Chiapas, who attacked the mass murder and maltreatment of
Indians by the conquistadores and declared that 'all people of the
world are men'.[6]

A different version of the pre-Adamite theory was developed by
Isaac La Peyrère (1596–1676), a Calvinist theologian born in Bor-
deaux, whose family were Marranos – Portuguese Jews forced to
conceal their faith by converting to Christianity, who had then fled to
France to escape continuing persecution by the Inquisition. In 1655
La Peyrère published a Latin volume *Prae-Adamitae*, translated into
English as *Men before Adam*, arguing that the world was already full
of human beings when God created Adam and Eve. Adam was the
father not of all humankind but only of the Jewish people, which had
been chosen by God to receive the divine law, and, through Jesus, to
bring redemption to all of humankind. Using pre-Adamism to argue
for tolerance, La Peyrère did not rank different types of humans in
any hierarchy. As an interpretation of Genesis this was highly pro-
vocative, and the book was burnt and its author arrested for heresy.
After a long interrogation and an interview with the Pope, La Peyrère
was forced to recant and convert to Catholicism. Passing the rest of
his life in retirement, he was unable to develop his ideas further.

In general, the function of pre-Adamite theories in the sixteenth
and seventeenth centuries was to legitimate the enslavement of indigenous peoples. Later these theories were reformulated in secular
'scientific' terms to become part of the intellectual armoury of modern racism. Figures such as the American physician, ethnographer
and 'craniologist' Samuel George Morton (1799–1851), argued on
the basis of supposedly scientific evidence that there were several species of humans with differently sized skulls and correspondingly

different levels of intellectual ability, with Africans being the least intelligent.

In late nineteenth-century Italy the criminologist Cesare Lombroso argued that criminal behaviour could be explained in terms of atavism or degeneracy – the innate tendency of some human beings to revert to a state of savagery – and asserted that white people were physically and intellectually superior to all other human beings. Lombroso was clear that he was continuing a current of thought that began in French Positivism, which aimed to ground the study of society in physiology. For Lombroso and many others, 'scientific racism' was an integral part of the Enlightenment.

Though twenty-first-century missionaries for 'Enlightenment values' resist the fact, modern racism emerged from the work of Enlightenment *philosophes*. Voltaire was a pivotal figure in this process. Unlike Hume and Kant, he made no contribution to philosophy. Few of the entries of his famous *Philosophical Dictionary* have to do with philosophical questions. He is significant chiefly as an embodiment of the Enlightenment mentality, which included a rationalist version of racism.

Voltaire seems never to have been an atheist. In an early poem he wrote that he had given up Christianity in order the better to love God, and while admiring the beautiful view from his country retreat exclaimed to a visitor: 'All-powerful God! I believe!' In the *Philosophical Dictionary* he observed: 'It at first appears to be a paradox, but examination proves it to be a truth, that theology often threw men's minds into atheism, until philosophy at length drew them out of it.'[7] There is no reason to think this was not Voltaire's sincere conviction.

While the greatest of the *philosophes* was no philosopher, his life revealed exceptional powers of thought. Born in Paris in 1694 and educated at a Jesuit college, Voltaire was in a literal sense self-made. His actual name was François-Marie Arouet. He adopted the title M. Arouet de Voltaire in 1718. The aristocratic 'de' hinted at a noble origin, though his family were solidly bourgeois (his father was an accountant). Since 'Voltaire' did not exist, François Marie-Arouet found it necessary to invent him. He died in 1778.

Using his new persona, Voltaire succeeded in becoming the man he wanted to be. Haunting the French court, enjoying for a time the attentions of Mme de Pompadour, hobnobbing with the 'enlightened despot' Frederick the Great, becoming the first modern best-selling author and making a fortune through a succession of bold business ventures, some of them shady, he became one of the most celebrated figures of the age. Avaricious and yet on occasion generous, assisting many in their misfortunes and struggles against injustice, ill with gout, scurvy, dropsy, herpes and a host of other ailments but always hard at work, he died a man of great wealth. His voluminous writings – which included lengthy histories and epic poems – have left little trace. Only *Candide*, an engaging satire on optimism in which Voltaire ridicules the claim of the German rationalist philosopher Gottfried Wilhelm Leibniz that ours is 'the best of all possible worlds', is read today.

Voltaire's racism was not simply that of his time. Like Hume and Kant, he gave racism intellectual authority by asserting that it was grounded in reason. In a letter he mocked the biblical account of a common human ancestry, asking whether Africans were descended from monkeys or monkeys from Africans. He gave the pre-Adamite theory a new twist when he suggested that Adamites belonged in an inferior species. All other human beings were pre-Adamites, though black people and others of colour were degenerate versions of the species, which was fully developed only in Europe. If European civilization was to flourish, it had to cleanse itself of Adamite influence, which meant returning to the values of the classical world before it had been corrupted by Jewish religion through Christianity.

Enlightenment thinkers today find the racism of its founding figures discomfiting. If they cannot deny the evidence, they will point to facts that seem to show the Enlightenment to be essentially benign. The French Revolution pronounced the universal rights of man – a declaration that on 28 January 1790 explicitly mentioned Jews as being entitled to the rights of 'active citizens'. How, then, could Enlightenment thinking harbour racism and anti-Semitism? Surely there is a paradox in the claim that the Enlightenment could be a vehicle for such poisonous notions: such ideas must emanate from the reactionary Counter-Enlightenment. In fact, modern secular anti-Semitism originated in the Enlightenment itself.[8]

More than anyone else, it was Voltaire who embedded

anti-Semitic prejudice in Enlightenment thinking. In an early work *Essai sur les Moeurs* written in the 1750s, he wrote of Jews: 'They kept all their customs, which are exactly the opposite of all proper social customs; they were therefore rightly treated as people opposed to all others, whom they served out of greed and hatred, out of fanaticism; they made usury into a sacred duty.' Voltaire's *Philosophical Dictionary* abounds in such statements. In the section on Abraham he describes Jews as 'a small, ignorant, crude people', adding that 'a man must be a great ignoramus or a great rascal to say that the Jews taught the Greeks.' The only things that are truly Jewish are 'their stubbornness, their new superstitions and their hallowed usury'. According to Voltaire, anything of value that may have emerged in Jewish life was borrowed from the Greeks or the Romans, the true sources of European civilization.

It is often suggested that Voltaire's anti-Semitism can be explained purely by his enmity to Christianity. As one leading scholar of the Enlightenment has put it, Voltaire 'struck at the Jews to strike at the Christians'.[9] It is true that his attacks on Jews were part of Voltaire's lifelong campaign against the Christian religion. But he also believed Christianity was an advance on the Jewish faith. For all its faults and crimes, Christianity contained something of the pagan civilization it had destroyed. Jewish religion (according to Voltaire) was inherently hostile to civilization, ancient or modern.

Voltaire's view of Jews expresses, in an extreme form, a theme that runs throughout the Enlightenment. Human beings become what they truly are only when they have renounced any particular identity to become specks of universal humanity. Certainly Jews could enter into the heavenly city of the eighteenth-century philosophers,[10] but only when they ceased to be Jews. Once this is understood, the riddle of Enlightenment anti-Semitism is solved.

Racism and anti-Semitism are not incidental defects in Enlightenment thinking. They flow from some of the Enlightenment's central beliefs. For Voltaire, Hume and Kant, European civilization was not only the highest there had ever been. It was the model for a civilization that would replace all others. The 'scientific racism' of the nineteenth and early twentieth centuries continued a view of humankind promoted by some of the greatest Enlightenment thinkers.

MESMERISM, THE FIRST
RELIGION OF SCIENCE

There have been many modern cults of science. The first was founded by Franz Anton Mesmer (1734–1815), a German doctor. Mesmer claimed to have discovered a universal energy, animal magnetism, which could be used to cure human disorders – physical, psychological and (for some of Mesmer's disciples) political. Mesmer promoted this theory through public healing sessions which attracted large audiences in Paris and Vienna. These sessions were held in luxurious establishments such as the Hôtel Bullion in Paris, where he created a seance-like atmosphere in the high-ceilinged, mirrored rooms where the sessions were held. Heavy drapes kept out noise and let in only a dim light. The healer and his patients communicated in whispers. These sessions inspired the format of later Spiritualist gatherings.

Mesmer also founded a secret society – the Society of Harmony – which attracted the support of prominent figures, including the Marquis de Lafayette, the French aristocrat who had achieved fame fighting in the American Revolution. It was the conspiratorial aspect of Mesmer's work that provoked official investigations into it. The French authorities were suspicious that Mesmerism might be a cover for subversive political activity. A group of doctors commissioned by Louis XV examined the practice of animal magnetism, reaching sceptical and negative conclusions. His work condemned and discredited, Mesmer fled into exile. Having spent his final years practising in Switzerland and Germany, he died almost forgotten. But his ideas lived on and have had a wide influence.[11]

The suspicions of the French authorities were not ungrounded. One of Mesmer's disciples applied the theory of animal magnetism in the cause of radical politics in the turmoil leading up to the French Revolution, declaring: 'A new physical world must necessarily be accompanied by a new moral world.'[12] But the political influence of Mesmer's ideas soon died away. In science and medicine they stimulated the study of hypnosis and psychosomatic illness. The impact of Mesmerism extended to other modern religions, such as Christian Science – whose founder Mary Baker Eddy denied any debt to Mesmer but was undoubtedly influenced by his work – and Theosophy, with Helena Blavatsky praising Mesmerism as a type of esoteric magic. Some have suggested parallels between Mesmer and Freud, since both seemed to be offering a technique of psychological healing.[13]

Mesmerism is the prototype for later ersatz religions such as Haeckel's Monism and Huxley's evolutionary humanism, which aim to use science to transform the human condition. With the aid of advancing knowledge the defects of human beings can be eliminated and their most admirable features enhanced. Human beings can, in effect, turn themselves into a superior species. But who decides what counts as such a species? Which actually existing humans will fashion the post-humans of the future? All cults of science confront the same unanswerable questions.

SCIENCE AND THE ABOLITION OF MAN

For Leon Trotsky, it was clear what a new-model humanity would be like. In a pamphlet published in 1924, he wrote:

> The human species, the coagulated *Homo Sapiens*, will once more enter into a state of radical transformation, and, in his own hand, will become an object of the most complicated methods of artificial selection and psycho-physical training ... It is difficult to predict the extent of self-government which the man of the future may reach or the heights to which he may carry his technique. Social construction and psycho-physical self-education will become two aspects of one and the same process ... Man will become immeasurably stronger, wiser and subtler; his body will become more harmonized, his movements more rhythmic, his voice more musical. The forms of life will become dynamically dramatic. The average human type will rise to the heights of an Aristotle, a Goethe, or a Marx. And above this ridge new peaks will rise.[14]

For some secular humanists, Trotsky's vision may seem inspiring even today. But what reason is there for choosing Aristotle, Goethe and

Marx (incidentally all male) as the model for a new kind of human being? Why are some human qualities more valuable than others?

In his essay 'Their Morals and Ours', published in 1938, Trotsky offered a 'scientific' reformulation of morality in terms of Marx's theory of class struggle. In this view all forms of ethical life are class-based; the highest is the one that serves the proletariat. Anything that promotes a proletarian revolution is justified – including the taking and shooting of hostages, a practice Trotsky pioneered in the Russian Civil War. Trotsky held this view of ethics throughout his life. In an essay first published in 1920, he attacked Marxists who shrank from employing terror as engaging in 'Kantian-priestly, Quaker-vegetarian chatter'.[15] Like Lenin before him, he believed that any means were justified if they promoted the right end. When Stalin dispatched one of his agents to kill Trotsky in exile in Mexico, where he was assassinated in August 1940, the Soviet leader doubtless believed that what he too had ordered to be done could be justified in these terms.

The problem is which ends to choose. Perhaps Trotsky thought there was no choice, and communism was the end-point of history that would come whatever he did. But unless you are ready to swallow Marx's philosophy of history, there is no reason for thinking this to be so. Even if communism was the predestined end of history, nothing would follow as to how anyone should live. Knowing that bourgeois civilization was doomed, a member of the bourgeoisie might still choose to fight for it to the end. That was the stance of the early twentieth-century Austrian economist Joseph Schumpeter, who thought socialism inevitable but found the prospect hideous. One person's end of history is another's hell on earth.

These difficulties reach well beyond Marxism and undermine the faith in progress that is the creed of secular thinkers today. If progress means a 'more advanced' version of the human species, how do we know what is more or less advanced?

This question was the subject of *The Abolition of Man*, a prescient little book by the linguist, theologian and writer of science fiction C. S. Lewis, first given as a lecture and published in 1943. Lewis argued that progressive thinkers who wanted to reshape society, and eventually the human species itself, had no way of deciding what progress meant. For many it involved increasing human power and using it to make Nature serve human ends. But the power of human-kind over Nature, Lewis pointed out, means in practice the power of some human beings over others. If society is planned so as to max-imize power over Nature, other human values will be crowded out. Anyone who cherishes these values will be on the receiving end of power, not exercising it.

The progressive thinkers of Lewis's day thought little of the average run of human beings. Like Trotsky, they believed they could design a better version of the human animal. After all, if most human beings are not just backward but obstacles to progress, what is the point of them? Surely it would be better to sideline these inferior specimens. The future belonged to a post-human species. The end-result of humankind remaking Nature was remaking humankind itself. As Lewis wrote, 'Man's final conquest has proved to be the abolition of man.'[16]

There were clear precedents for Lewis's view. In 1923, the bio-chemist J. B. S. Haldane had published a widely read essay, *Daedalus: or, science and the future*, where he wrote, 'We must not take tradi-tional values too seriously.'[17] Haldane believed a new ethic was needed that was grounded in science. He said little about what such an ethic might be, though a period as a member of the Communist Party and some years as an agent of Soviet military intelligence may supply clues. In a short book, *The World, the Flesh and the Devil: an enquiry into the future of three enemies of the rational soul*, first published in 1929, the distinguished crystallographer J. D. Bernal – like Haldane, an admirer of Stalin – went further, looking forward to a future in which human beings would cease to be separate bio-logical organisms and be 'completely etherealized' into a ray of light.

A post-human future was welcomed by many progressive thinkers in Lewis's time. Today the abolition of man is welcomed by thinkers calling themselves transhumanists.

TRANSHUMANISM AS TECHNO-MONOTHEISM

In his book *The Singularity is Near: when humans transcend biol-ogy* (2005), the futurologist Ray Kurzweil looks forward to an explosive advance in science that will enable humans to transcend the physical world and thereby escape death. It is telling that both Bernal and Kurzweil take the titles of their books from the Bible – Bernal's echoing a passage in the New Testament (Letter to the Ephesians 2:1–3), Kurzweil's echoing John the Baptist's 'The Kingdom of Heaven is near' (Matthew 3:2). Knowingly or otherwise, both of them are suggesting that transhumanism is religion recycled as science.

Transhumanists believe human beings are essentially sparks of consciousness, which can escape mortality by detaching themselves from the decaying flesh in which they happen to be embodied. Deriving from mystical philosophies such as Platonism and Gnosticism, it is an idea at odds with scientific materialism. For a genuine materialist – the Roman poet-philosopher Lucretius, for example – there can be no question of the human mind severing its links with the material world. The mind is itself material and dies when the body dies.

Transhumanists reply that technologies not available in Lucretius' time will allow the mind to be uploaded into cyberspace. But it is unclear whether what will be uploaded will be a conscious mind, or just a spectral app spun off from the contents of the brain. Even if consciousness can be detached from the human body in which it was initially embodied, the mind will still depend on a substratum of matter. The rejuvenated cadavers that emerge from cryonic suspension will be physical objects, as will be the cyborgs to which some transhumanists imagine their minds being transferred. Disembodied minds floating in cyberspace would not escape this dependency. If something like cyber-consciousness comes into being, it will be an artefact of physical objects – computers and the networked facilities they need. If this material infrastructure is destroyed or disrupted, any minds that had been uploaded will be snuffed out. Cyberspace is a projection of the human world, not a way out of it.

At bottom, the transhumanist movement is a modern variant of the dream of transcending contingency that possessed mystics in ancient times. Gnostics and disciples of Plato longed to be absorbed in a timeless Absolute, a refuge from the ugly conflicts of the human world. They understood that this refuge could be entered only if they shed their individuality, and practised asceticism and contemplation in an effort to erase their personal identities and desires. Less intelligent than their ancient precursors, contemporary transhumanists imagine they can become immortal on terms of their own choosing. Like Dostoevsky's character Kirillov, who is discussed in Chapter 5, they believe that since there is no God they must become gods themselves.

Transhumanism is a contemporary version of a modern project of human self-deification. One of the few to recognize this is the Israeli historian of science Yuval Noah Harari. In *Sapiens: a brief history of humankind*, first published in Hebrew in 2011, and *Homo Deus: a brief history of tomorrow* (2016), Harari suggests that the expanding powers that humankind is acquiring through the advance of science could end up bringing about human extinction. Using bio-engineering and artificial intelligence, the human species will enhance its physical and mental capacities far beyond their natural limits. Eventually it will turn itself into God. 'In the twenty-first century,' Harari writes, 'the next big project of humankind will be for us to acquire the divine powers of creation and destruction, and upgrade *Homo sapiens* into *Homo Deus*.'[18]

Unlike Bernal and Kurzweil, Harari accepts that the new God that humankind has created may be indifferent to human beings. At that point, 'human history will come to an end and a completely new process will begin.'[19] This poses a question Bernal and Kurzweil forgot to ask. Why should a post-human species have any value for humans? Possibly these transhumanist thinkers believe a universe containing such a species would be a better place. Henry Sidgwick, whose work was considered in the last chapter, wrote that ethics meant seeing the world from 'the point of view of the universe'.[20] But, unless some presiding Deity is imagined, the universe has no point of view. In that case why should humans want to make way for successor-species, no matter how much cleverer they may be? Equally, why should a superhuman species fashioned by humans bother about its creators?

Harari is aware of these questions. Yet his history of the future rests on a confusion. 'Humanity' is not going to turn itself into God, because 'humanity' does not exist. All that can actually be observed is the multifarious human animal, with its intractable enmities and divisions. The idea that the human species is a collective agent, setting itself 'big projects' and pursuing them throughout history, is a humanist myth inherited from monotheism. Harari oscillates between talking of humankind playing God and humans becoming like gods. These are very different futures, and only the latter has any credibility. If it ever comes about, a post-human world will not be one in which the human species has deified itself. More like the polytheistic cosmos imagined by the ancient Greeks, it will be ruled by a warring pantheon of gods. Anyone who wants a glimpse of what a post-human future might be like should read Homer.

Like the evolutionary process that produced the human species, post-human evolution will be a process of drift. If superhuman or post-human species appear they will be created by governments and powerful corporations, then used by any group that can get its hands on them – criminal cartels, terrorist networks, religious cults and the like. Over time, these new species will be modified and redesigned – first by their human controllers, then by the new species themselves. It will not be too long before some of them slip free from their human creators. One type may come out on top, at least for a while. But there is nothing to suggest the emergence of a god-like being supreme over all the rest. There will be as many types of post-humans as there are human groups interested in fashioning them.

As the post-human species that humans have created mutate and evolve, human history may indeed come to an end. The question remains why transhumanists find this prospect so appealing. Is it because they think humankind is only a channel for values that transcend the human animal, such as knowledge or information? But, unless you posit a Platonic heaven beyond the material universe, it is hard to know where these values are to be found. They are not features of the natural world. If such values are to have any claim on humans, they must have value for humans.

Transhumanist philosophies make sense only as versions of evolutionary theology. Since the universe does not contain a God from whose point of view a post-human species could be valuable, such a Deity must be inherent – so these unwitting theologians believe – in the evolutionary process itself. Kurzweil writes:

Evolution moves toward greater complexity, greater elegance, greater knowledge, greater intelligence, greater beauty, greater creativity and greater levels of subtle attributes such as love. In every monotheistic tradition God is likewise described as all of these qualities, only without any limitation: infinite knowledge, infinite intelligence, infinite beauty, infinite creativity, infinite love, and so on. Of course, even the accelerating growth of evolution never achieves this infinite level, but as it explodes exponentially it certainly moves rapidly in that direction. So evolution moves inexorably towards this conception of God, though never quite achieving this ideal.[21]

It is a vision at odds with Darwin's theory of natural selection. If any god emerges from evolution, it can only be by a process of artificial selection – in other words, by humans deciding to create it. But a man-made God could evolve to be like the Demiurge of the Gnostics, malignant or careless in its treatment of humankind.[22]

Luckily nothing like this will ever occur. Not because the technologies will not work. Humans may well use science to turn themselves into something like gods as they have imagined them to be. But no Supreme Being will appear on the scene. Instead there will be many different gods, each of them a parody of human beings that once existed.

4

Atheism, Gnosticism and Modern Political Religion

Seemingly opposed, utopian dreams of a perfect world and faith in gradual improvement have the same source in Christian monotheism. The idea of progress is a mutant version of the Christian belief that human salvation is found in history, while modern revolutionary and liberal movements continue the faith in an end to history that inspired the teaching of Jesus. Partisans of revolution, reform and counter-revolution think they have left religion behind, when all they have done is renew it in shapes they fail to recognize.

While the largest formative influence has been Christianity, modern politics has also been shaped by an older way of thinking. A powerful current in many religions, philosophies and political movements, Gnosticism – mentioned in earlier chapters discussing the origins of Christianity and modern humanism – is the belief that humans can be delivered from a dark world by the saving light of knowledge. There have been many ancient and modern views of the nature of this deliverance. (In one interpretation, the biblical Genesis myth can be read as a criticism of the ancient Gnostic belief in salvation through knowledge.) But the Gnostic impulse remains the same. When the twentieth-century scientist J. D. Bernal looked forward to the human animal 'etherealizing' itself to become 'a ray of light', he was renewing a Gnostic vision. Ray Kurzweil's dream of uploading the human mind into cyberspace expresses the same Gnostic faith.

Gnostic ways of thinking are found in many cultures, but modern Gnosticism is a distinctively western phenomenon. A belief in salvation through knowledge is part of the western tradition. Plato believed freedom came with entering a mystical realm beyond the cave. If he was as Plato represented him, Socrates thought goodness and truth were one and the same. But it would never have occurred to them to imagine that this harmony could be realized in the course of history. Christianity was needed to turn Gnosticism into the explosive political force that it became in the modern west.

If you want to understand modern politics, you must set aside the idea that secular and religious movements are opposites. Since they aimed to extinguish the influence of religion in society, Jacobinism and Bolshevism were secularizing forces; but both were channels for the millenarian myths of apocalyptic Christianity. In that it rejected with contempt the egalitarian morality professed (if rarely consistently applied) by Enlightenment thinkers, Nazism was a Counter-Enlightenment movement. But when they tried to create a 'science of man' based in physiology, the Nazis continued an Enlightenment project. Liberalism emerged in the seventeenth century as the application of a universal morality inherited from monotheism; but from John Stuart Mill onwards it became a vehicle for the religion of humanity, which aimed to replace monotheism even as it continued monotheistic thinking in another guise. Islamist movements are expressions of religious fundamentalism; but they are also shaped by western ideologies such as Leninism and fascism, which were themselves partly shaped by religion.

The belief that we live in a secular age is an illusion. If it means only that the power of the Christian churches has declined in many western countries, it is a description of fact. But secular thought is mostly composed of repressed religion. The idea of a secular realm originated in Jesus teaching his disciples to render unto Caesar what is Caesar's. It is Jewish and Christian monotheism – not the European Enlightenment – that is the chief source of the practice of toleration. But monotheism also inspired many of the anti-liberal movements of modern times. A mix of Christian notions of redemption with a Gnostic belief in the salvific power of knowledge has propelled the project of salvation through politics. With the revival of religion in recent times, we may seem to be living in a post-secular era. But since secular thinking was not much more than repressed religion, there never was a secular era.

MILLENARIANISM AND GNOSTICISM
IN THE WESTERN TRADITION

Modern revolutionary movements are continuations of medieval millenarianism. The myth that the human world can be remade in a cataclysmic upheaval has not died. Only the author of this world-transforming end-time has changed. In olden times, it was God. Now it is 'humanity'.

In his seminal work *The Pursuit of the Millennium*, first published in 1957, Norman Cohn summarized the defining features of millenarian movements:

Millenarian sects or movements always picture salvation as

(a) collective, in the sense that it is to be enjoyed by the faithful as a collectivity;

(b) terrestrial, in the sense that it is to be realized on this earth and not in some other-worldly heaven;

(c) imminent, in the sense that it is to come both soon and suddenly;

(d) total, in the sense that it is utterly to transform life on earth, so that the new dispensation will be no mere improvement on the present but perfection itself;

(e) miraculous, in the sense that it is to be accomplished by, or with the help of, supernatural agencies.[1]

With the exception of the last, all these features are replicated in modern revolutionary movements. From the French Jacobins in the late eighteenth century through the Bolsheviks and the followers of Mao and Pol Pot in the twentieth century, these revolutionaries believed humankind was fashioning a new world. In ancient times, Gnostics imagined that individual adepts could free themselves from the prison of matter by ascending to another realm of being. Possessed by an even more fantastical vision, modern Gnostics imagine that another realm can be built on Earth.

Eric Voegelin, a leading twentieth-century scholar of Gnosticism, summarized the Gnostic way of thinking in six ideas. First, Gnostics are dissatisfied with their situation in the world; second, they explain their discontent by asserting that the world is inherently malformed; third, they believe salvation from the current order of things is possible; fourth, they assert that this order will have to be transformed in an historical process; fifth, they believe this transformation can be achieved by human effort; and lastly, this change requires deploying a special kind of knowledge, which the Gnostic adept possesses.[2]

The six features that Voegelin identified can be found in modern types of Gnosticism. But he was mistaken in suggesting that Gnosticism has always featured the belief that the order of being can be changed in an historical process. Throughout most of its history, Gnostics have thought of salvation as an escape from history. Even when Gnosticism was blended with apocalyptic myth (as it was in some sects that were active around the time of Jesus) Gnostics did not believe the world could be improved, only destroyed in a cataclysmic end-time conflict. The belief that the world can be transformed in an historical process is found only in modern Gnosticism and was inherited from Christianity.

A more accurate summation of Gnostic thinking can be found in the works of the German scholar Hans Jonas. Gnosticism posits a radical discontinuity between humankind and God, Jonas writes:

> The deity is absolutely transmundane, its nature alien to that of the universe, which it neither created nor governs and to which it is the complete antithesis: to the divine realm of light, self-contained and remote, the cosmos is opposed as the realm of darkness . . . the transcendent God himself is hidden from all creatures and is unknowable by natural concepts. Knowledge of him requires supranatural revelation and illumination and even then can hardly be expressed otherwise than in negative terms.

Gnostic cosmology is dark and paranoid: 'The universe . . . is like a vast prison whose inmost dungeon is the Earth, the scene of man's life. Around and above it the cosmic spheres are ranged like concentric enclosing shells.' The human soul is 'benumbed, asleep or intoxicated by the poison of the world: in brief, it is "ignorant".'

Salvation means leaving the world: 'The goal of gnostic striving is the release of the "inner man" from the bonds of the world and his return to his native realm of light . . . Equipped with gnosis, the soul after death travels upwards . . . reaches the God beyond the world and becomes reunited with the divine substance.' Complete liberation comes only after death.[3]

The belief that the human world could be remade on a better plan is found nowhere among the ancient Gnostics. Why Voegelin insisted on identifying Gnosticism with this idea is not clear. Perhaps he wanted to believe that the west is innocent of the monstrous political religions of modern times. But Gnosticism is hardly alien to western traditions. Interacting with Christian millenarian myths, Gnosticism created the secular religions that fashioned the modern world.

JAN BOCKELSON'S MÜNSTER: AN EARLY MODERN COMMUNIST THEOCRACY

When he described Bolshevism as a religion rather than 'an ordinary political movement', Bertrand Russell hit on a larger truth. Because they shared some of the myths of monotheism, the great modern political experiments have been religious in nature. This can be seen by considering the millenarian movements of early modern times.

At the end of his study, Cohn writes:

> It is characteristic of this kind of movement that its aims and premises are boundless. A social struggle is seen not as a struggle for limited, specific objectives, but as an event of unique importance, different in kind from all other struggles known to history, a cataclysm from which the world is to emerge totally transformed and redeemed. This is the essence of the recurrent phenomenon – or, if one will, the persistent tradition – that we have called 'revolutionary millenarianism'.[4]

The links between this millenarian tradition and modern revolutionary movements become clearer when one considers the early modern Anabaptist prophet Jan Bockelson. In the autumn of 1534,

Bockelson – also known as John of Leyden, where he had been a leader of the Anabaptist movement, a radical Christian insurgency that rejected the authority of the Church – declared himself king of the German city of Münster. He ruled over a communist theocracy that lasted until June 1535, when after a long siege the city was taken by forces loyal to the Church and he was tortured to death in the town square.

Bockelson did not use religion to deceive and exploit others. Like many secular prophets who came after him, he was possessed by the visions he preached. Nor was the faith of his followers instilled only by fear. For a time, they were gripped by an authentic apocalyptic frenzy. When Bockelson first arrived in Münster in the spring of 1533 it was already a theocratic-communist city-state. Under the leadership of Jan Matthys, who became Bockelson's mentor, the Anabaptists sacked the cathedral and burnt the books in its library. Announcing that true Christians held money in common, Matthys ordered all gold and silver coins to be handed over to the public authorities. From then on, money was to be used only for purposes such as buying supplies, distributing propaganda and hiring mercenaries. Communal dining halls were set up where people could eat together while listening to Bible readings. Food hidden in private houses was requisitioned. Later private life itself was condemned, and it was decreed that doors and windows be open at all times day and night. Matthys's rule ended when, acting on what he believed was a divine command, he left the city on Easter Sunday in 1534 with a small band of followers to confront the army that was besieging the city, only to be captured and killed. His dismembered body and private parts were nailed to the city's gate.

Seizing power after Matthys's death, Bockelson took the communist city-state to a new level. Labourers became the property of the city; any artisan who was not conscripted into the army became a public employee. After a period of heavily policed puritanism, a radical form of polygamy was enforced. All women over a certain age were compelled to marry. Any who refused to take additional husbands were threatened with – and in some cases suffered – execution. A type of sexual communism was enforced in which everyone – but women in particular – was considered the sexual property of everyone else. Denying anyone their marital rights became a capital offence. As we will see in Chapter 5, a similar regime of sexual common ownership was advocated over two centuries later by the Marquis de Sade.

When Bockelson proclaimed himself king he had a role in mind that went beyond ordinary monarchy. He would be the messiah of the last days, and rule throughout the world. This came to him as a divine revelation. In May 1534, he ran naked through the city streets seemingly unable to speak. After three days he revealed God's guidance: the old ways of the city were to be replaced by a new dispensation. In September, he declared himself the messiah foretold in the Old Testament prophecies – the king of the New Jerusalem. More than a city ruled by an inspired prophet, Münster was to be the beginning of a new world.

Bockelson changed life in the city beyond recognition. Streets and gates were renamed, Sundays and feast days abolished. Lutherans and Catholics were expelled, leaving their money, food and spare clothes behind them. Those who remained were rebaptized in lengthy ceremonies in the market-place. Failing to undergo the ceremony was punishable by death. Along with enforcing a new calendar, Bockelson installed a system whereby he decided the names of newborn children. Replacing the feast days of the past, public banquets were instituted. A throne was erected in the market-place, where the king would distribute small loaves of bread to the people.

While he staged these feasts, Bockelson ruled the city by terror. Unauthorized meetings were forbidden on pain of death. Anyone who now attempted to leave the city, or helped others to do so, was at risk of being beheaded. One of the purposes served by the terror was the protection of the state from subversion by agents of the Church. But soon the executions became a kind of popular theatre. The king presided over the performance and often performed the beheading, after which the cadavers were quartered and the pieces exhibited at spots around the city. By June of 1535, when Bockelson was killed, these public spectacles had become daily events.

Following Bockelson's death, radical Anabaptism went into decline. Another messianic leader emerged to found another New Jerusalem in Westphalia. Like Bockelson's, it practised communism in goods and women (the leader had twenty-one wives). Lasting over a decade, the commune degenerated into a robber band and subsisted on the proceeds of theft until the new messiah was captured and executed along with many of his disciples. Communities descended from the Anabaptists continued to be founded, some – such as the Mennonites – surviving to the present day. But the attempt to take the heavens by storm died out among Christian believers by the end of the sixteenth century. Thereafter apocalyptic myths renewed themselves in explicitly political forms, most of them militantly secular.

JACOBINISM, THE FIRST MODERN POLITICAL RELIGION

The Jacobins form the clearest link between medieval millenarians and twentieth-century revolutionary movements. The French reign of terror was more than an 'aristocide' of the privileged classes. As would be the case later in Bolshevik Russia, the largest numbers of casualties by far were common people. The victims included those who were killed in the suppression of a popular counter-revolutionary rising in the Vendée that broke out after the execution of King Louis XVI in January 1793 and continued until its defeat in 1796. Around a third of the population perished in the region, where the methods of repression used by the revolutionary forces included burning crops, razing villages and mass drowning. The human cost of the French Revolution runs into hundreds of thousands of lives. Producing leaders such as Maximilien Robespierre, who as a member of the Committee for Public Safety orchestrated the execution of around 20,000 enemies of the revolution in Paris and was himself guillotined in 1794, the Jacobins acted on the maxim – formulated by Robespierre himself in a speech to the National Assembly – 'Pity is treason.'

Like the Anabaptists, the Jacobins were anxious to preserve their new regime from the assaults of counter-revolutionary forces. Again like the Anabaptists, their attempt to erase the human traces of the old order also obeyed a religious passion. An early nineteenth-century French liberal captured this development when he described the Revolution as 'a political revolution which functioned in the manner and which took on in some sense the aspect of a religious revolution'. The revolution operated, Alexis de Tocqueville continued,

> in relation to this world, in precisely the same manner that religious revolutions function in respect to the other; it considered the citizen in an abstract fashion, apart from particular societies, in the same way that religions consider man in general, independently of time and place. It sought not merely the particular rights of French citizens, but the general political rights and duties of all men. Accordingly, since it appeared to be more concerned with the regeneration of the human race than with the reformation of France, it generated a passion which, until then, the most violent political revolutions had never exhibited. It could therefore assume that appearance of a religious revolution that so astonished contemporaries; or rather it became itself a kind of new religion, an imperfect religion it is true, without a form of worship, and without a future life, but one which nevertheless, like Islamism, inundated the earth with soldiers, apostles and martyrs.[5]

This is a penetrating insight into the transformation of politics into religion that gathered pace in the nineteenth and twentieth centuries. Contrary to Tocqueville, however, the Revolution did acquire forms of worship and an idea of a future life. Jacobinism produced the first modern political religion. The forms of worship were secular, and the future life an imaginary earthly paradise.

That Jacobinism was a religion was fully acknowledged by Jacobins themselves. Starting soon after the storming of the Bastille in July 1789, a succession of festivals announced the founding of a new civic cult. In November 1793 – year 2 in the new calendar – a Feast of Reason was held throughout the country. Churches were turned into Temples of Reason, and a ceremony held in Notre Dame Cathedral in which a Goddess of Reason was installed on a newly erected altar (the original one having been demolished) clothed in flowing Roman-style robes to which tricolour sashes had been added. A programme of dechristianization was enforced throughout France. Churches were closed, and statues, crosses and inscriptions removed from graveyards. The aim was not the separation of Church and state but the destruction of Christianity and its replacement by a new state cult.

The Jacobins were not all of one mind as to the nature of the cult they had established. Some veered towards atheism: it was the very idea of God that had to be stamped out. Others tended to the Deist creed, in which God has created the world but does not intervene in it. Among the latter was Robespierre, who at the height of his power in 1794 announced the foundation of the Cult of the Supreme Being.

An official declaration in May of that year set out the tenets of the new religion:

> The French people recognise the existence of the Supreme Being and the immortality of the soul. It recognises that the worship worthy of the Supreme Being is the practice of the duties of man. It places in the front rank of these duties to detest bad faith and tyranny, to respect the weak, to defend the oppressed, to do unto others all possible good and to be unjust to no one. There shall be instituted fêtes in order to remind man of the Divinity and of the dignity of his being. These fêtes shall take their names from the glorious events of our Revolution, the virtues most cherished and most useful to man, and the great gifts of nature.[6]

This civic religion was the proto-version of the religion of humanity later formulated by Saint-Simon and Comte. Today Comte's religion of humanity frames the orthodoxies of secular humanism. All of these modern creeds have mixed monotheistic ways of thinking with elements derived from Gnosticism. One of the most instructive examples of this fusion is Bolshevism.

BOLSHEVISM: MILLENARIAN HOPES, GNOSTIC VISIONS

It may seem a long way from a sixteenth-century theocratic city-state to the Soviet experiment in communism that began in 1917. Yet there are some interesting affinities between the two. Lenin believed the overthrow of Tsarism was not just a particular upheaval; the Russian Revolution would inaugurate a new world. Like the Anabaptist theocracy in Münster, the Bolshevik regime marked the birth of the new order by changing the names of cities, streets and public places and instituting a new calendar. Churches and synagogues, mosques and temples, were sacked, any valuables they contained looted and the buildings demolished or put to other uses. A new economic system – War Communism – was imposed based on direction of labour and rationing and aiming to abolish money and market exchange. Once it had been established in Russia, Lenin expected that the new order would spread throughout the world.

Bolshevism was composed from a number of traditions, some of them distinctively Russian. According to the Orthodox theologian Nikolai Berdyaev, 'In virtue of their religious-dogmatic quality of spirit, Russians are always apocalyptic or nihilist.'[7] Berdyaev traced Bolshevism back to the revolution-from-above imposed by Peter the Great and the Russian myth of being a Third Rome that would redeem the world. As will be seen below, Bolshevism also contained a strand of Gnosticism influenced by Russian Orthodoxy. But in addition the Bolsheviks continued a European tradition, coming from the Jacobin civic religion, which used methodical terror in order to purge society of the past. Bolshevism belonged in a lineage going back to medieval millenarianism.

Despite many claims to the contrary, the methodical use of terror began with Lenin not Stalin, who employed Lenin's methods on a larger scale. In his 'Hanging Order' of August 1918, Lenin instructed Bolsheviks to execute peasants who resisted grain requisitioning by public hanging 'so that the people might see and tremble'.[8] Orders to provincial Soviets included directives to 'shoot and deport' sex workers who were distracting Red Army soldiers from their duties. In 1919, all of Moscow's Boy Scouts were shot and in 1920 all members of the lawn tennis club put to death. Prominent figures who were expected to be hostile to the new regime were expelled from the country. In 1922, Lenin hired two German steamers in which hundreds of philosophers, linguists, theologians, writers and ballerinas were transported out of the country, others following in trains.[9] The safety of those who refused to leave was not guaranteed.

Lenin practised terror on a vast scale. The repression that followed the workers' revolt in Kronstadt and a peasant rebellion in Tambov in 1920–21 involved tens of thousands of executions.[10] Nikolai Gumilev, co-founder of the avant-garde Acmeist movement in poetry and husband of the celebrated poet Anna Akhmatova, was arrested by the Cheka – the Soviet secret police – for complicity in a supposed monarchist conspiracy and, along with sixty other supposed conspirators, shot in a forest in August 1921. The Tambov rebellion was crushed by methods that included destroying entire villages, deporting the inhabitants and using poison gas to clear the forests where others had fled. Peasants who were captured suffered summary execution by methods that included sexual mutilation, impalement, freezing, scalding and – as in the French Terror – mass drowning.

The scale and severity of Bolshevik repression is often put down to the Civil War that was raging at the time. The Whites engaged in mass killing, including massacring Red Army forces and murdering around 300,000 Ukrainian and Belorussian Jews. But Lenin's terror served a goal that extended far beyond the Civil War. Along with securing the survival of his new regime, it aimed to purge Russia of the human remnants of the past – a goal stated in a founding text of the Soviet state.

In the Declaration of the Rights of Toiling and Exploited People promulgated in the Soviet Union in January 1918, sections of the population designated as 'former people' were disenfranchised. The disenfranchised groups included functionaries of the Tsarist police and military, class aliens who lived off unearned income, clergy of all religions and anyone economically dependent on any of these. Debarred from the rationing system (for many the chief source of sustenance), liable to have their property confiscated and prohibited from seeking public office, people in these groups were excluded from society. This applied not only to former persons but also to their families. Many of these 'sedentary elements' died of starvation. Many others were consigned to the gulag concentration camps. By 1920, the Cheka was operating over twenty camps, where many 'former persons' died of overwork, beatings or cold. As in the French Terror, most of the casualties of revolution were ordinary people.

The majority of the inmates in the camps were not from the old ruling or middle classes. According to official statistics collected at the time, around 80 per cent were illiterate or had little schooling. The largest numbers by far of the victims of Bolshevik terror were peasants or industrial workers.[11]

For Lenin the human cost of the Revolution was a passing incident on the way to a new world. He based his belief, which he seems to have held until his death, on his own version of Marx's interpretation of history, which he expounded in pamphlets written in hurried intervals in his struggle for power. But other currents of thought entered into Bolshevism, including some that were unmistakably Gnostic.

It is well known that Lenin's body was embalmed for display in a public mausoleum. Less well known is that Lenin's tomb was the work of a Bolshevik grouping calling themselves 'God-builders', which included the writer Maxim Gorky, the commissar of enlightenment Anatoly Lunacharsky (a disciple not only of Marx but also of Nietzsche), who controlled education and censored the arts in the early years of the Soviet regime, and the first Soviet trade minister Leonid Krasin.

These God-builders believed that with the continuing advance of science Lenin might actually be revived at some point in the future. They were influenced by the religious thinker Nikolai Fedorov (1829–1903), who believed science could deliver the freedom from death promised in Orthodox Christianity, which understood immortality as meaning physical resurrection in a perfected human body. Overcoming mortality demanded that humankind should seize control of the natural world, and ultimately leave the planet for other worlds (an idea of Federov's that has influenced Russian space research up to the present day). Long before the visionaries of Silicon Valley, Russian God-builders promoted a technological project of liberation from death.

Speaking at the funeral of a fellow revolutionary three years before Lenin's death on 21 January 1924, Krasin expounded a Bolshevik version of Federov's philosophy. Future revolutionary leaders need not die for ever:

I am certain that a time will come when science will become all-powerful, that it will be able to recreate a deceased organism. I am certain that the time will come when one will be able to use the elements of a person's life to recreate the physical person. And I am certain that when that time will come, when the liberation of mankind, using all the might of science and technology, the strength of which we cannot now imagine, will be able to resurrect great historical figures – I am certain that when that time will come, among the great historical figures will be our comrade.[12]

It was Krasin who proposed that the Soviet leader be immortalized in a public mausoleum. To that end he attempted to freeze Lenin's cadaver using a refrigeration system. The system did not work, and Lenin's body began to show signs of decomposition. So another refrigerator was ordered from Germany – for the Bolsheviks, the home of the most advanced technology – but it too failed to arrest the process of putrefaction. It was only when these early attempts at cryonic suspension had proved unsuccessful that Lenin's corpse was finally embalmed.

Initially made of wood, Lenin's tomb was opened to the public in August 1924. The cubic structure was conceived by the architect A. V. Shchusev, a member of the Constructivist movement who also redesigned the Lubyanka prison. At a meeting of the commission set up to organize Lenin's funeral, Shchusev explained how the cubic tomb would immortalize the dead leader: 'Vladimir Illich is eternal . . . How shall we honour his memory? In architecture the cube is eternal . . . Let the mausoleum, which we will erect as a monument to Vladimir Lenin, derive from a cube.'

Shchusev's cubist design was inspired by Kazimir Malevich, founder of the Suprematist movement in art. Believing abstract geometrical forms were signs of a higher reality, Malevich viewed the cubic structure of Lenin's mausoleum as representing a realm beyond death. 'The point of view that Lenin's death is not death, that he is alive and eternal,' Malevich wrote, 'is symbolized in a new object, taking as its form the cube.' The artist went on to propose that Lenin's followers install a cube in the corner of their homes, offices, factories and farms. The Party accepted the proposal, and ordered the manufacture and distribution of the cubes. For a time, 'Lenin corners' containing the cubes could be found throughout the country.

Lenin's final resting-place was a glass case in a red granite mausoleum completed in the autumn of 1930. When Nazi forces were advancing on Moscow in July 1941, Lenin's body was evacuated before any of the city's inhabitants. After the war he returned to the mausoleum. In 1973, when the Party decided to produce a new set of official documents, Lenin's was the first Party card to be reissued. Until the Soviet state collapsed, his clothes were regularly changed for new suits made by a team of KGB seamstresses.[13]

The care shown to Lenin's cadaver contrasted with the indifference to human life shown by Lenin himself. Under his leadership the Bolsheviks practised a type of mass killing that had not been known before in Russia. They killed not only to defeat their many enemies but in order to fashion a new humanity. In this they were treading a path that had been followed not only by the Jacobins but before them by millenarians like Bockelson. The messiah of Leyden did not care how many died in building the New Jerusalem. Beyond redemption, they were destined for damnation. Lenin had no such beliefs. But he was more than willing to kill systematically, and on an enormous scale, to create the new world envisioned in the ersatz religion of Bolshevism.

BOCKELSON, HITLER AND THE NAZIS

Friedrich Reck-Malleczewen is not someone whose name will be immediately recognized. For the few who know of him today, he was an aristocratic Prussian army officer and author of *Diary of a Man in Despair*, a ferocious denunciation of Hitler and Nazism, who was arrested on his estate in October 1944 and some months later died in the Dachau concentration camp. But Reck-Malleczewen was also the author of a lesser-known work, a study of Anabaptist Münster he called *Bockelson: a tale of mass insanity*. In the entry in the *Diary* for 11 August 1936, he wrote:

I have been working on my book about the Münster city-state set up by the Anabaptist heretics in the sixteenth century. I read accounts of this 'Kingdom of Zion' by contemporaries, and I am shaken. In every respect, down to the most ridiculous details, that was a forerunner of what we are now enduring . . . As in our case, a misbegotten failure conceived, so to speak, in the gutter, became the great prophet, and the opposition simply disintegrated, while the rest of the world looked on in astonishment and incomprehension . . . As with us, the masses were drugged; folk festivals, useless construction, anything and everything, to keep the man in the street from a moment's pause to reflect . . .

The fact that the Münster propaganda chief, Dusentschnur (*sic*), limped like Goebbels is a joke which history spent four hundred years preparing . . . A few things have yet to happen to complete the parallel. In the besieged Münster of 1534, the people were driven to swallow their own excrement, to eat their own children. This could happen to us too, just as Hitler and his sycophants face the same inevitable end as Bockelson . . .[14]

The *Diary* testifies to the author's hatred and contempt for Hitler and the Nazi regime. For Reck-Malleczewen, a self-styled nobleman who converted to Catholicism in 1933 because he believed the Church offered the strongest bulwark against the modern world, Nazism embodied a revolt of the 'mass-man' that began in the French Revolution. In October 1944, he wrote of 'the insanity which has spread from 1789 on, in whose flames Europe will be consumed – and which could only burn so destructively because the milder flame of a generalised European intellectuality, the flame of those who seek God on this earth, has been extinguished . . . I have been born too early on this planet. I will not survive this insanity.'[15]

These forebodings were well founded. Despite taking precautions such as burying pages of the *Diary* in constantly changing hiding-places in the woods of his estate, Reck-Malleczewen was arrested twice by the SS. The role of enemy of the modern world he had chosen for himself had not endeared him to the Nazis, many of whom regarded themselves as thoroughly modern. After the first arrest he was released, but after the second he was sent to Dachau.

When and how he died there is not known. He may have perished of disease, or been shot in the back of the head. Either way, his premonition of his end was fulfilled some time in the early months of 1945.

Reck-Malleczewen saw many common features in the sixteenth-century theocratic dictator and the Nazi leader – even their faces, he wrote more than once, looked alike. The deeper affinity was in the apocalyptic hopes the two men embodied. Both of them owed their appeal not to promises of specific reforms, or even to a new type of social order, but to a vision of the end of the world. Since a new world could come into being only as a result of a catastrophe, destruction on a vast scale was an integral part of their mission. Reck-Malleczewen was not alone in noting the kinship between Bockelson and Hitler. Eva Klemperer, the wife of the diarist of the Nazi years Victor Klemperer, made the same comparison.[16]

The Nazis could not have achieved the levels of popular support they did without the devastation of 1914–18, mass unemployment, hyperinflation, the national humiliation inflicted in the Versailles peace settlement and the collusion of elements in Germany's existing political elites. But Nazism was not an 'ordinary political movement', however extreme. Like Bolshevism – though in different ways – Nazism channelled old-style apocalyptic religion into a new kind of politics.

The name of the Nazi regime, the 'Third Reich', comes from medieval apocalyptic myth. The twelfth-century Christian theologian Joachim of Flora divided history into three ages, ending with a perfect society. Taken up by the Anabaptists during the Reformation, the idea of a Third Reich surfaced again in the work of the inter-war 'revolutionary conservative' Moeller van den Bruck, who looked to the establishment of a millennium-long new German order in his book *The Third Empire* (1932), which sold millions of copies.

Alongside these millenarian currents, Nazism was a vehicle for 'scientific racism'. The emergence of this ideology in the French Enlightenment was noted in the last chapter, while its development in the work of Ernst Haeckel was discussed in Chapter 2. The genocidal policies that culminated in the Holocaust have a long pedigree in German thought. The belief that Germany needed 'living-space', which was invoked to legitimate Hitler's policies of eastwards expansion, was popularized by the ethnographer Friedrich Ratzel (1844–1904), who promoted it using ersatz-Darwinian ideas. When Germany expanded into Africa, 'racial science' was again invoked, this time to legitimate policies of extermination.

The near-extermination of the Herero and Nama indigenous people of South West Africa (now Namibia) between 1904 and 1907 was publicly debated in the Reichstag and justified in terms of scientific theories of racial hierarchy. When these peoples revolted, they were slaughtered. Those who tried to escape – as some did to the British territory of Bechuanaland, where those who survived the journey were given sanctuary – were also killed wherever possible. Concentration camps were established where most of the inmates died from disease and overwork. The camps were also sites for medical experiments, including some in which inmates were injected with arsenic in order to study their reactions. Herero women were required to boil the heads and clean the skulls of inmates who had died or been executed so that the remains could be dispatched to German universities to be studied.

Far from these shipments being kept secret, they were celebrated. For some years a colour postcard circulated in Germany showing how the skulls were packed. A number of the leading doctors involved in these experiments returned from Africa to teach in Germany, where they transmitted theories and methods that would be employed in the Nazi period. Dr Eugen Fischer, who oversaw the work on the skulls, was a mentor of an anti-Semitic doctor who pioneered research on twins, among whose students was Josef Mengele.[17]

In combining apocalyptic myth with racist pseudo-science the Nazis brought together some of the worst elements in German thought and culture. That Nazism was an indigenously German phenomenon is important. 'Revisionist' historians have suggested that the Nazi genocide of Jews 'copied' Soviet crimes.[18] This is a fundamental error. Both Nazi Germany and the Soviet Union aimed to fashion a new world by methods that included killing sections of humanity. But there is a crucial difference between being killed as part of a campaign of terror, as in the Soviet Union, and being marked out for certain death in a campaign of extermination, as Jews were by Nazis and their collaborators in European countries and German-occupied Soviet Russia. Simple numerical comparisons pass over this distinction. At their height, Soviet camps may have incarcerated a larger proportion of the population than camps in Nazi Germany, and many of the inmates perished. Yet, however hard it was to survive in them, Soviet camps were not designed to kill inmates within days or hours of their arrival. The Nazi Holocaust remains an incomparable crime.

Some in the Nazi elite may have gloried in their readiness to practise systematic extermination. Boasting they had gone further in rejecting Jewish and Christian values, they believed it showed them to be more authentic revolutionaries than the Bolsheviks. In a 1943 novel *Arrival and Departure*, Arthur Koestler, who in his travels across Europe as a covert agent of the Soviet-controlled Communist International (Comintern) talked with many Nazi ideologues, put into the mouth of one of his characters this Nazi confession of faith:

> Don't you realise that what we are doing is a real revolution and more internationalist in its effects than the storming of the Bastille or the Winter Palace in Petrograd? . . . We have embarked on something – something grandiose and gigantic beyond imagination. There are no more impossibilities for man now. For the first time we are attacking the biological structure of the race. We have started to breed a new species of *homo sapiens*. We are weeding out its streaks of bad heredity. We have practically finished the task of exterminating or sterilising the gipsies in Europe; the liquidation of the Jews will be completed in a year or two . . . We are the first to make use of the hypodermic syringe, the lancet and the sterilising apparatus in our revolution.[19]

Koestler's fictional Nazi ideologue had many real-life counterparts. All of them were clear that in rejecting Jewish and Christian monotheism they were also rejecting liberal values. In this regard they were closer to the truth than secular humanists today, who refuse to acknowledge the theistic origins of modern liberalism.

EVANGELICAL LIBERALISM

When modern liberalism first appeared cannot be decided in any clear-cut manner. There have always been many liberalisms, not just one, and it is normal for self-described liberals to deny the title to others who belong in the same tradition. Like every creed, liberalism is prone to the narcissistic divisions that come from minor differences. However, John Locke (1632–1704) provides a widely agreed starting point for modern liberal thinking. Locke's thought is indebted to Christianity at every point, and his liberalism is a clear and direct descendant from monotheism.

According to Locke, humans were free because they had been created by God with the capacity to direct their course in life. Human rights were not free-standing moral facts but grounded in human duties to God. In practice, not all human beings were protected by rights. Locke believed that the indigenous peoples of America had no right to the lands they inhabited because they had left them in a state of wilderness. He excluded atheists from toleration because he believed they had no reason to honour their promises. But consistently applied or not, Locke's liberal values were grounded in monotheistic premises.

The same was true of Kant. He believed a universal moral law could be grounded in reason. By asking what moral judgements they are ready to apply universally, human beings would formulate principles that apply to everyone. But the belief that everyone who follows this method will come up with the same principles is not based on observation (in fact they do not). As Kant's more sceptical disciple Schopenhauer pointed out, you will think of morality in terms of universal laws only if you believe there is a divine law-giver.

Modern liberalism attempts to ground a universal moral law on non-theistic foundations. John Stuart Mill tried this by arguing that the human animal is a progressive species. But even if humankind was a species of this kind the fact would not secure a future for liberal values, since liberty might be useful only at some stages of human progress. Freedom of inquiry might be useful only for as long as knowledge had not advanced to a point where ethics and politics became scientific disciplines. Once that point had been reached, liberty would be redundant, as Auguste Comte believed.

Mill was horrified by this prospect, writing to his companion Harriet Taylor that Comte's project amounted to 'liberticide' and describing Comte's system of thought in his *Autobiography* as 'the completest system of intellectual and temporal despotism, which ever yet emanated from the human brain'. In his striking but nowadays little-read essay *Auguste Comte and Positivism* (1865), Mill attacked Comte's 'inordinate demand for "unity" and "systematization"' and denounced the illiberal tendencies in Comte's thought:

> One of the doctrines which M. Comte most strenuously enforces in his later writings is that, during the preliminary evolution of humanity, terminated by the foundation of Positivism, the free development of our forces of all kinds was the important matter, but that from this time forward the principal need was to regulate them. Formerly the danger was of their being insufficient, but henceforth of their being abused. Let us express, in passing, our entire dissent from this doctrine.[20]

The vehemence of these attacks shows that Comte had exposed tensions in Mill's thinking. As he made clear in the essay *On Liberty*, Mill believed liberty applied only to 'human beings in the maturity of their faculties' – a category that excluded not only children but also 'backward states of society'. Like other liberals of his time, Mill never evinced any doubt that colonial government of the kind practised by Britain and other European states served the cause of human progress. But if liberty had no application in backward states of human development, why should it have any permanent place in advanced societies? If the goal was progress towards the greatest happiness, liberty would dwindle in value as knowledge of the most effective means to happiness increased. The end-result would be an illiberal society of the kind Comte admired and Mill loathed, where power was held by experts and freedoms of thought and lifestyle were curbed in the interest of continuing progress.

Following a Gnostic way of thinking, the French savant believed a new 'science of man' would enable perennial dilemmas of ethics and politics to be resolved. Having imbibed a monotheistic faith that history is a process of human redemption, he was convinced that humankind was advancing towards this end. A mix of Gnostic and Christian myths shaped Comte's religion of humanity, and shapes the liberal mind today.

Having renounced theism, liberal thinkers have concocted grand theories in which their values are the end-point of history. But the sorcery of 'social science'[21] cannot conceal the fact that history is going nowhere in particular. Many such end-points have been posited, few of them in any sense liberal. The final stage of history for Comte was an organic society like that which he imagined had existed in medieval times, but based in science. For Marx, the end-point was communism – a society without market exchange or state power, religion or nationalism. For Herbert Spencer, it was minimal government and worldwide laissez-faire capitalism. For Mill, it was a society in which everyone lived as an individual unfettered by custom or public opinion.

These are very different end-points, but they have one thing in common. There is no detectable movement towards any of them. As in the past the world contains a variety of regimes – liberal and illiberal democracies, theocracies and secular republics, nation-states and empires, zones of anarchy and all manner of tyrannies. Nothing suggests that the future will be any different.

This has not prevented liberals from attempting to install their values throughout the world in a succession of evangelical wars. Possessed by chimerical visions of universal human rights, western governments have toppled despotic regimes in Afghanistan, Iraq and Libya in order to promote a liberal way of life in societies that have never known it. In doing so they destroyed the states through which the despots ruled, and left nothing durable in their place. The result has been anarchy, followed by the rise of new and often worse kinds of tyranny.

Liberal societies are not templates for a universal political order but instances of a particular form of life. Yet liberals persist in imagining that only ignorance prevents their gospel from being accepted by all of humankind – a vision inherited from Christianity. They pass over the fact that liberal values have no very strong hold on the societies in which they emerged. In leading western institutions of learning, traditions of toleration and freedom of expression are being destroyed in a frenzy of righteousness that recalls the iconoclasm of Christianity when it came to power in the Roman empire. If monotheism gave birth to liberal values, a militant secular version of the faith may usher in their end.

Like Christianity, liberal values came into the world by chance. If the ancient world had remained polytheistic, humankind could have been spared the faith-based violence that goes with proselytizing monotheism. Yet, without monotheism, nothing like the liberal freedoms that have existed in some parts of the world would have emerged. A liberal way of life remains one of the more civilized ways in which human beings can live together. But it is local, accidental and mortal, like the other ways of life human beings have fashioned for themselves and then destroyed.

5

God-haters

THE MARQUIS DE SADE AND THE
DARK DIVINITY OF NATURE

'Imperious, choleric, irascible, extreme in everything, with a disso-
lute imagination the like of which was never seen, atheistic to the
point of fanaticism, there you have me in a nutshell, and kill me or
take me as I am, for I shall not change.'[1] This self-description gives a
remarkably accurate picture of the Marquis de Sade. Forever associated with cruelty – the term 'sadism' was coined as a late
nineteenth-century derivation from his name – Donatien Alphonse
François, Marquis de Sade (1740–1814), opposed the excesses of the
French Revolution, including the use of capital punishment, while
urging the revolutionaries to go further in rejecting traditional sexual morality. His reputation is that of a devoted libertine, and his
writings abound in descriptions of orgies. But there is little suggestion of pleasure in these debauches, which feature highly ritualized
fantasies of torture, incest, coprophagy and sexual murder, and serve
mainly as occasions for lengthy disquisitions on morality and
religion.

Sade's ruling passion was not sex, or cruelty. More than by any
other impulse, he was driven by hatred of God. He was if not the
first, then certainly the greatest modern prophet of misotheism – the
current of thought that hates God as the enemy of humanity. It is
Sade's misotheism together with his strikingly original view of
Nature that makes him worth reading today. He wanted his life and
ideas to be forgotten. 'When the grave has been filled in,' he instructed

in his will, 'it will be sown with acorns so that eventually all traces of my tomb may disappear from the earth, just as I like to think my memory will be effaced from the minds of men.'[2]

Sade's dream of disappearing from history was not realized. He will always be an infamous figure. But he was also a serious atheist thinker, who exploded for ever the notion that a good life could be achieved by following natural human impulses.

Even for his time Sade's life was eventful. Born into an aristocratic French family that could trace its title of nobility back to the early twelfth century, he always displayed a highly developed capacity for self-assertion:

> Connected by my mother with the highest in the land; by my father with all that was most distinguished in Languedoc; born in Paris in the midst of luxury and self-indulgence, I believed as soon as I could think that nature and fortune had joined together to cover me with gifts. I believed this because people had been foolish enough to say so to me and this absurd prejudice made me haughty, despotic, and quick to anger; it seemed to me that the whole world should give way to my caprices and that it was only necessary to form them for them to be satisfied.[3]

Sade put this self-portrait into the mouth of Valcour, one of the protagonists of his novel *Aline et Valcour*, which he wrote while imprisoned in the Bastille in the 1780s. It could apply just as well to Sade himself. In the autumn of 1763 he was arrested for 'scandalous debauchery', which seems to have involved the flagellation of prostitutes, and was imprisoned in the fourteenth-century Château de Vincennes on the outskirts of Paris, where he would later spend many years.

At the time Sade had not revealed the furious enmity to religion that runs through all of his writings. So it may not be surprising to find him writing contritely from prison to the chief of police:

> Unhappy as I am here, I do not complain, I deserved the vengeance of God and feel it; to bemoan my sins and weep over my faults are my

only employ. Alas, God could have annihilated me without giving me time to repent; what thanks must I give Him for allowing me to return to the fold. Sir, I pray you to allow me the means to accomplish this by permitting me to see a priest. Through his good offices and my own sincere repentance, I hope soon to be fit to approach the holy Sacraments, whose complete neglect was the first cause of my fall.[4]

A priest was sent to him, but if Sade returned to the fold it was not for long. He had uncounted sexual liaisons, including one with his wife's sister and a public relationship with a celebrated courtesan, whom he took to live with him for a time in his chateau. These relationships did not sate his desires. In 1768 he became involved in a major scandal arising from his having flogged an impoverished widow, cut her flesh with a knife and poured hot wax into the wounds. He claimed the widow consented to this mistreatment in exchange for money. She claimed she was tricked into submitting to it in the belief that she would obtain a position as housekeeper.

To avoid penalties Sade, by then in prison in Lyons, used his influence and that of his mother-in-law at Court to obtain a *lettre de cachet* – a royal licence enabling men of noble birth to escape punishment for their crimes by being imprisoned without trial and then released. After six further months in prison he was freed on condition that he would not live in Paris, or in other large cities, in future. By this time his relations with his wife seem to have improved, and he spent much of the next four years with her at the family castle in La Coste.

A later scandal left Sade a fugitive on the run from execution. In June 1772, he travelled to Marseilles with a manservant to arrange an orgy. In the course of the proceedings, which involved four girls and Sade himself being whipped and sodomized by his manservant, he offered the girls sweets laced with aphrodisiacs. They declined the offer or ate only sparely, but a woman he visited later consumed large quantities of the sweets and was violently sick for some days.

The upshot was that an order was issued for Sade's arrest, he and his manservant were condemned to death for poisoning and sodomy and the two of them were executed in effigy. Sade escaped by leaving the country, accompanied by his wife's sister, who was by now his lover. It may have been this more than any other event that turned his influential mother-in-law into a deadly enemy. Sade's wife, on the other hand, sided with her husband. Disguised as a man, she visited him in prison in Italy, and throughout his later periods of incarceration back in France would bring him food, books and other necessities.

Most of Sade's later years were passed in places of confinement. Lacking exercise, he became enormously fat, and at times displayed symptoms of the madness of which he was often accused. He became obsessed with numbers. During flagellation sessions he would keep an exact tally of the strokes he had inflicted and received. In a note to his daughter he wrote: 'This letter has 72 syllables corresponding with the 72 weeks of my imprisonment; it has 7 lines and 7 syllables, which are exactly the 7 months and 7 days from April 17th to January 22nd 1780.'[5] He developed delusions of reference, finding 'signals' in letters and plots against him among those who were close to him. As sometimes happens, these paranoid fantasies contained grains of truth – Sade's mother-in-law was in fact plotting against him, for example. He found some meaning in his sequestered existence by putting on theatrical performances, and tried to establish himself as a playwright. His motives were partly financial, since in the later decades of his life he was always hard up and at times virtually penniless.

When the Revolution erupted in 1789 Sade welcomed it. He may have had a small part in starting the rebellion. By that time there were only seven prisoners in the Bastille, where he was being held. On 2 July he was denied his daily walk on the tower, where guns were being prepared to deal with disorder in the streets below, and he shouted to passers-by that prisoners were being killed. The next day he was moved to an asylum. Eleven days later, the almost deserted Bastille was stormed. The Revolution followed, with more severe repression and much greater loss of life than at any time during the *ancien régime*.

Sade responded to these events in *Yet Another Effort, Frenchmen, If You Want to be Republicans!*, a pamphlet he inserted into *Philosophy in the Bedroom* (1795), a novel presented in the form of dialogues. He argues for the prohibition of religion – 'No more gods,

Frenchmen,' he proclaims, 'no more gods, lest under their fatal influence you wish to be plunged back into all the horrors of despotism' – and the abolition of 'the atrocity of capital punishment'. Killing another human being could be justified, he suggests, if the act is driven by passion but not by the 'cold and impersonal' processes of law. Sade also promoted sexual communism, arguing that women were, in effect, a type of property that should be distributed according to principles of equality.

During the Terror, Sade's life was at risk because his name was wrongly included in a list of counter-revolutionary émigrés, and his chateau was pillaged. Following some years of liberty he was arrested in 1800, apparently because he was planning to publish *Juliette*, a work deemed utterly immoral. Still incarcerated, he died in December 1814 aged seventy-four. He had laid down in his will that he should be buried without ceremony or mourning. In the event he was given a Christian burial and a cross was planted on the grave.

In all, Sade would spend nearly thirty years of his life in one kind of prison or another, the last thirteen in an insane asylum. It was while he was locked up in Vincennes that he wrote the first of his works that can be identified with reasonable certainty, *A Dialogue between a Priest and a Dying Man* (1782), in which the atheist philosophy from which he would never deviate was clearly set out.

The dying man, standing in for Sade himself, tells the priest he wants to repent. What he repents is not the sins he has committed, however, but the fact that he did not commit more of them. His only reason for regret is that he made so little use of the capacity for pleasure that Nature had given him. Seeing himself as a disciple of Nature, he wishes he had followed her commands more faithfully. He has no fear of the oblivion that comes with death, since Nature will give him a kind of immortality. Nothingness, he tells the priest, is:

> neither dreadful nor absolute ... Before my eyes have I not the example of Nature's perpetual generations and regenerations? Nothing perishes in the world, my friend, nothing is lost; man today, a worm tomorrow, the day after tomorrow a fly ... And what entitles me to be rewarded for virtues that are in me through no fault of my own, or punished for crimes wherefore the ultimate responsibility is

not mine? . . . We are the pawns of an irresistible force, and never for
an instant is it within our power to do anything but make the best of
our lot and forge ahead along the path that has been traced out for us.
There is not a single virtue that is not necessary to Nature and con-
versely not a single crime which she does not need . . .

Since the priest is not persuaded by this reasoning, the dying man
calls in six women, 'lovelier than the light of day', who are waiting in
the next room in order to pleasure him in his last hours and who pro-
ceed to minister to the cleric as well. After receiving their attentions
the priest is converted to the dying man's philosophy, becoming 'one
whom Nature has corrupted, all because he had not succeeded in
explaining what a corrupt nature is'.[6]

This early piece is typical of Sade's writings in its didactic tone.
Sade writes to convert his readers from their deluded faith in a
benevolent Deity. 'The idea of God', he wrote, 'is the sole wrong for
which I cannot forgive mankind.'[7] That he describes this belief as
unforgivable shows the depth of his hatred of religion. It also shows
that he never ceased to be religious.

In her essay 'Must We Burn Sade?' Simone de Beauvoir wrote,
'Sade's nature was thoroughly irreligious.'[8] She misread him. Though
he sometimes pretended to laugh at the idea of God, he was in fact
possessed by it. Rightly, de Beauvoir dismissed the disquisitions Sade
put in the mouths of his debauched protagonists as materialist ped-
antry: 'Instead of an individual voice, all one hears is the droning
drivel of Holbach and La Mettrie.'[9] She was referring to Julien
Offray de La Mettrie (1709–51) and the Baron d'Holbach (c. 1723–
89), who viewed human beings as complex machines governed by the
pursuit of their own pleasure. If humanity renounced religion and
followed the promptings of Nature, these materialist thinkers
believed, the result would be a far happier world. In the enlightened
circles of his time, these views were commonplace. But Sade's version
of materialism sounded a new and more sombre note. Hating the
Christian God, he also hated Nature, cursing it even as he obeyed
what he believed were its laws.

A dispassionate view of Nature showed it to be indifferent to happiness, human or otherwise. Incessant predation, destruction and

death are the natural order of things. In view of these facts, Sade posed a question: should not the enlightened individual, liberated from religious delusions, accept this order and revel in it? By doing so, he or she will find pleasure, even as the species as a whole remains sunk in suffering. Causing others to suffer could produce an excitement far beyond any achieved through mere debauchery.

Expositions of this sombre materialism fill many pages of Sade's writings. A couple of passages of dialogue, taken almost at random from *Juliette*, capture the flavour of his peculiarly wilful and cerebral hedonism. Conversing with a libertine philosopher, by trade a public executioner, Juliette asks him: 'Am I correct in believing that it is only with the aid of libertinage you succeed in vanquishing unnatural prejudice?' The philosopher-executioner replies:

> It is no longer contested, Madame, that libertinage leads logically to murder; and all the world knows that the pleasure-worn individual must regain his strength in this manner of committing what fools are disposed to call a crime: we subject some person or other to the maximum agitation, its repercussion on our nerves is the most potent stimulant imaginable, and to us are restored all the energies we have previously spent in excess. Murder thus qualifies as the most delicious of libertinage's vehicles, and as the surest . . .[10]

Later Juliette expatiates on the pleasure she derived from a famine that broke out in the vicinity of her chateau:

> Everything that could move a heart of stone was submitted to my tranquil gaze: it got them nowhere, steadfast I remained; weeping mothers, naked infants, ghostlike figures wasted by hunger, I simply smiled . . . The logic of the thing was eminently simple: I reaped pleasure merely from denying to the destitute the wherewithal that would have brought them respite; ah, what might I not experience from being the direct and sole cause of that destitution? If, said I, it is sweet to refuse to do good, it must be heavenly to do evil.[11]

The end-point of Sade's libertinism was the pursuit of evil for its own sake. He makes this explicit when, in *The 120 Days of Sodom*, he has a bishop declare: 'The doctrine which must perpetually govern our conduct is: the more pleasure you seek in the depth of crime the more frightful the crime must be.' One of the bishop's interlocutors responds:

> There are but two or three crimes to perform in this world, and they, once done, there's no more to be said; all the rest is inferior, you cease any longer to feel. Ah, how many times, by God, have I not longed to be able to assail the sun, snatch it out of the universe, make a general darkness, or use that star to burn the world! Oh, that would be a crime, oh yes, and not a little misdemeanour such as are all the ones we perform that are limited in a whole year's time to metamorphosing a dozen creatures into lumps of clay.[12]

For Sade's libertines, sexual murder is too trifling a crime to be truly pleasurable. Nothing but a world-destroying act could sate their passions. They pursue, not pleasure in itself, but instead the satisfaction that comes from doing evil.

It should be clear by now that Sade's rebellion is essentially religious. It is also thoroughly confused. Sade's libertines have rebelled against the God of monotheism in order to serve the divinity of Nature. But if everything human beings do is natural, how can religion be singled out as being contrary to Nature? Prayer is no less natural than sex, virtue as much as vice. If everything humans do is ordained by Nature, they are following Nature when they obey morality and convention. In the *Dialogue between a Priest and a Dying Man*, Sade accused religion of corrupting natural humanity. But what counts as corruption? Like Satan in Milton's *Paradise Lost*, Sade's motto is 'Evil, be thou my good.' Yet if everything that is natural is good, there can be no evil.

Sade believed his atheism supported a republican ethic of equality. In *Yet Another Effort, Frenchmen, If You Want to be Republicans!*, he wrote that republicanism dictated sexual communism:

> If then it becomes incontestable that we have received from Nature the right indiscriminately to express our wishes to all women, it likewise becomes incontestable that we have the right to compel their

submission ... Has Nature not proven that we have that right, by
bestowing upon us the strength needed to bend women to our will?[13]

Later in the pamphlet he suggests – inconsistently – that women
should exercise similar rights over men. In a footnote, he writes that
he is not suggesting one become the property of another, only that
each has the right to enjoy the other.

Along with many other Enlightenment writers of the time, Sade
supports his demands for radical changes in sexual morality by cit-
ing the customs of other cultures. The ancient Greeks instituted
regular orgies for the benefit of the citizenry, he notes. But the diversity of mores cannot show that any one way of living is the best. Sade
writes that a woman 'existing in the purity of Nature's laws' cannot
object to being forced to satisfy the desires of men, since in that condition 'she definitely belongs to all men'. It is the ties of marriage and
exclusive relationships based on love ('the soul's madness') that are
unnatural.[14] But, once again, if everything that humans do is natural, so are the bonds created by love. If Nature has any lesson to
teach, it is only that humans can find satisfaction in many ways.

Sade's originality is not in his ugly utopia, a theocratic version of
which had been instituted by Jan Bockelson two centuries earlier in
Münster, but in his terrifying vision of Nature. This is best expressed
in *Justine, or the Misfortunes of Virtue* and *Juliette, the Prosperity of
Vice*, which appeared in their final forms only in 1797 and were not
freely published in France until the early 1960s. Here Nature appears
not as a benign teacher of virtue but as a malevolent goddess that
delights in destruction. 'Nature has elaborated no statutes, instituted
no code; her single law is writ deep in every man's heart: it is to satisfy
himself, deny his passions nothing, and this regardless of the cost to
others.'[15] Not only does Nature sanction the most extreme egoism.
She inspires in human beings the lust for destruction that she herself
embodies. 'Never will too many or enough murders be committed on
earth, considering the burning thirst Nature has for them.'[16]

Sade is emphatic that obeying Nature will not bring happiness:

Disgust with life becomes so strong in the soul that there is not a
single man who would want to live again, even if such an offer were

made on the day of his death . . . yes, I abhor Nature; and I detest her because I know her well . . . I have experienced a kind of pleasure in copying her foul deeds. What a contemptible and odious being to make me see daylight only in order to have me find pleasure in every-thing that does harm to my fellow men . . . Should I have such a mother? No; but I will imitate her, all the while detesting her. I shall copy her, as she wishes, but I shall curse her unceasingly . . .[17]

The speaker is a character in *Juliette*, but it is hard to believe these sentiments were not those of Sade himself. In a well-known essay on 'Juliette, or Enlightenment and Morality', Theodor Adorno and Max Horkheimer wrote that in the Sadean world 'Torture becomes the essential truth and a happy life vanity.'[18] The Marxian philos-ophers meant this to apply to the human world. But for Sade it was a true account of the cosmos. A happy life was vanity because Nature had condemned him to torment.

Sade was mistaken when he imagined he had left monotheism behind. Instead he changed one unforgivable deity for another. If he raged against the God of Christianity for creating a world abound-ing in evil, he railed with equal violence at the malevolent goddess of Nature that he had invented. Only someone reared in Christian monotheism, and unable to shake it off, could have adopted such a stance.

When they advised returning to Nature, Epicureans were recom-mending tranquil detachment from the human world. When Nature was presented as a pitiless machine by the Italian poet Leopardi, who despite being brought up as a good Catholic seems to have shed Christianity completely, he suggested that this vision should inspire compassion. For atheists who truly leave monotheism behind, there is no problem of evil. As a result they can enjoy an equanimity that Sade never achieved, or perhaps desired.

The implication of atheism is that the world simply exists and requires no author. Yet Sade could not do without some kind of agency that could be held to account for his own misery and (though this was less important for him) that of his fellow human beings. Rejecting the Christian God as evil, he turned to Nature; but evil returned in the form of the dark goddess he had invented. His solution was to rebel against Nature even as he obeyed the destructive impulses it had implanted in him.

IVAN KARAMAZOV HANDS
BACK HIS TICKET

One of Dostoevsky's Russian contemporaries, the critic and social reformer Nikolai Mikhailovsky, described the writer as 'a cruel talent'. The critic had in mind, to begin with, the psychological torment to which the narrator of Dostoevsky's short novel *Notes from Underground* (1863) subjects Liza, a prostitute with whom he is acquainted. Mikhailovsky writes:

> There are no reasons for his spite towards her, the underground man foresees no results from his tormenting ... the hero torments her because he wants or likes to torment. There is no cause or purpose here, and, according to the author, they are not needed, for there is an unconditional cruelty, a cruelty *an und für sich* (for its own sake), and that is precisely what is interesting.[19]

The existence of motiveless cruelty was one reason Dostoevsky rejected the rationalist philosophies by which he had been attracted in his youth, along with many other Russian intellectuals of his generation. Born in 1821, he joined in his twenties a circle of radical intellectuals in St Petersburg who were captivated by French utopian socialist theories. A police agent who had infiltrated the group reported its discussions to the authorities. On 22 April 1849 Dostoevsky was arrested and imprisoned with the other members. After some months of investigation they were found guilty of planning to distribute subversive propaganda and condemned to death by firing squad. The punishment was commuted to a sentence of exile and hard labour, but the tsar's authority to decree life or death was confirmed by forcing the prisoners to undergo a mock execution.

In a carefully stage-managed charade Dostoevsky and the rest of the group were taken on the morning of 22 December 1849 to a regimental parade ground, where scaffolding had been constructed and decorated with black crepe. Their crimes and sentence were read out, an Orthodox priest asked them to repent and three men were tied to stakes in readiness for execution. At the last moment there was a roll of drums, and the firing squad lowered its rifles. Reprieved from death, the prisoners were put in shackles and sent into Siberian exile – in Dostoevsky's case for four years of hard labour, followed by compulsory service in the Russian army. In 1859 a new tsar allowed Dostoevsky to end his Siberian exile. A year later he was back in the literary world of St Petersburg.

Dostoevsky's experience altered him for ever. He did not abandon his view that Russian society needed to be radically changed. He continued to believe serfdom was immoral, and to the end of his life detested the landed aristocracy. But his experience of being on what he had believed to be the brink of death had given him a new perspective. Many years later he remarked, 'I cannot recall when I was ever as happy as on that day.' From then onwards he realized that human life was not a movement from a backward past to a better future, as he had believed or half-believed when he shared the ideas of the radical intelligentsia. Instead, every human being stood at each moment on the edge of eternity. Following this epiphany, Dostoevsky rejected for ever the rationalism to which he had been drawn as a young man.

He was scornful of the ideas he found in St Petersburg when he returned from his decade of Siberian exile. The new generation of Russian intellectuals was gripped by a mélange of European philosophies. French materialism, German humanism and English Utilitarianism were melded together into a peculiarly Russian combination that came to be called 'Nihilism'.

Today a nihilist is commonly understood as someone who believes in nothing. The Russian Nihilists of the 1860s were very different. They were fervent believers in science, who wanted to destroy religion so that a better world than any that had hitherto existed could come into being. Nihilism of this kind was the creed of most of those who rejected religion throughout the nineteenth and twentieth centuries. Whether they realize it or not, it remains the creed of most secular thinkers today.

Dostoevsky rejected this rationalist faith. Human beings are nothing like the rational animals imagined by philosophers. They are not guided in their lives chiefly by motives either of self-interest or of concern for the general welfare. Their actions express their impulses, which include not only a desire for cruelty for its own sake but also a desire for freedom.

Addressing the intelligentsia to which Dostoevsky himself had once belonged, the narrator of *Notes from Underground* asks mockingly:

> you want to cure man of his old habits and improve his will according to the demands of reason and common sense. But how do you know not only whether it's possible, but even if it's *necessary* to remake him in this way ... After all, perhaps man likes something other than well-being? Man loves to create and build roads, that's indisputable. But why is he also so passionately fond of destruction and chaos? ... Why are you so firmly, so triumphantly convinced that only the normal and positive – in short, only well-being – is advantageous to man? Perhaps he loves suffering just as much? Perhaps suffering is just as advantageous to him as well-being?[20]

Progressive thinkers imagined a new world could be constructed by using human reason. Dostoevsky did not imagine anything like this was possible. But he loathed what he believed pursuing it would bring. 'You believe in the crystal palace, eternally indestructible, that is, one at which you can never stick out your tongue furtively nor make a rude gesture ... Well, perhaps I'm so afraid of this building precisely because it's made of crystal and it's eternally indestructible, and because it won't be possible to stick one's tongue out even furtively.'[21]

Notes from Underground was the first major book Dostoevsky wrote after returning from Siberia. It was partly directed against a utopian novel, *What is to be Done?*, by the Russian radical writer Nikolai Chernyshevsky. But *Notes from Underground* had another source in a trip Dostoevsky made to London in 1862 as part of a two-and-a-half-month European tour of Germany, France, England, Switzerland and Italy. In *What is to be Done?* Chernyshevksy had one of his characters dream of the Crystal Palace that had been constructed in London for the Great Exhibition of 1851. It is not clear whether he saw the Palace when he visited London in 1859 to meet Alexander Herzen, but for Chernyshevsky it embodied the modern faith in reason and progress. During his eight days in London, Dostoevsky did visit it. He recorded this experience in an essay, *Winter Notes on Summer Impressions*, published in February 1863 in *Vremya* (*Time*), a journal of which he was then editor. He found London horrifying:

> A city as unfathomable as the ocean, bustling day and night; the screech and roar of machines; railroads passing over houses (and soon under them, too); that boldness of enterprise, that apparent disorder which is actually bourgeois orderliness in the highest degree; that polluted Thames; that air saturated with coal dust; those splendid commons and parks; those terrible sections of the city like Whitechapel, with its half-naked, savage and hungry population. A city with its millions and its worldwide commerce, the Crystal Palace, the International Exposition ... Ah yes, the Exposition is astonishing ... It is all so solemn, triumphant and proud that you gasp for breath. You look at these hundreds of thousands, these millions of people humbly streaming here from all over the face of the earth – people come with a single thought, quietly, relentlessly, mutely throurning through this colossal palace, and you feel that something has taken place, that something has come to an end.[22]

In *Notes from Underground*, Dostoevsky's impressions of the Crystal Palace were used in a satirical assault on the Nihilist thinkers of his time. A key part of their philosophy was the belief that human life is governed by 'laws of nature'. Human beings do not choose to be cruel or kind; they simply manifest these qualities in accordance with natural laws. Both the gall-ridden underground man and the pitiful target of his cruelty are governed by these laws. In the underground man, the result is not killing for its own sake as in Sade, but mere nastiness – the sordid pleasure that comes with humiliating another human being. In Dostoevsky's *Demons*, however, Nihilist philosophy is shown leading to suicide and murder.

Published in 1872, the book has been attacked for being didactic in tone. There can be no doubt that Dostoevsky wanted to show that the dominant ideas of his generation were harmful. But the story he tells is also a comedy, cruelly funny in its depiction of high-minded intellectuals toying with revolution without knowing anything of what it means in practice. The plot is a version of actual events that unfolded as Dostoevsky was writing the book. A former teacher of divinity turned terrorist, Sergei Nechaev, was arrested and convicted of complicity in the killing of a student. Nechaev had authored a pamphlet, *The Catechism of a Revolutionary*, which argued that any means (including blackmail and murder) could be used to advance the cause of revolution. The student had questioned Nechaev's policies, and so had to be eliminated.

Early English translations of the novel were titled 'The Possessed' – a misreading of a Russian word better rendered as 'demons'. However, the earlier title was closer to Dostoevsky's intentions. Though at times he is unsparing in his portrayal of them, it is not the revolutionaries who are the demons of the novel. The demons are the ideas by which the revolutionaries are possessed. For Dostoevsky, none of these ideas was more important than atheism.

Dostoevsky depicts this state of possession in the character of Alexei Nilych Kirillov, a member of a secret revolutionary society in the small provincial town where the action of the novel is set. In order to liberate humanity from the fear of death that follows from the loss of any belief in God, Kirillov has decided to kill himself. Like Nietzsche, who invented the superman as a successor to Christ, he sees himself as a redemptive figure who can deliver humankind from meaninglessness.

Kirillov explains:

There was one day on earth, and in the middle of the earth stood three crosses. One on a cross believed so much he said to another: 'This day you will be with me in paradise.' The day ended, they both died, went, and did not find either paradise or resurrection. What had been said would not prove true. Listen: this man was the highest on all the earth, he constituted what it was to live for. Without this man the whole planet with everything on it is – madness only. There has not been one like *Him* before or since, not ever, even to the point of miracle. This is the miracle, that there has not been and never will be such a one. And so, if the laws of nature did not pity even *This One*, did not pity even their own miracle, but made Him, too, live amidst a lie and die for a lie, then the whole planet is a lie, and stands upon a lie and a stupid mockery. Then the very laws of the planet are a lie and a devil's vaudeville . . .

. . . It is my duty to proclaim unbelief . . . Man has done nothing but invent God, so as to live without killing himself; in that lies the whole of world history up to now. I alone for the first time in world history did not want to invent God . . . To recognise that there is no God, and not to recognise at the same time that you have become God, is an absurdity, otherwise you must necessarily kill yourself . . . But one, one who is first, must necessarily kill himself, otherwise who will begin and prove it? It is I who will necessarily kill myself in order to begin and prove it . . . it is my duty to believe that I do not believe . . . I have found it: the attribute of my divinity is – Self-will![23]

Kirillov signs a letter in which he assumes responsibility for the murder of a student, believed to be a police informant, who had been killed by the revolutionary group. Then, as promised, he shoots himself dead. The co-conspirator to whom he explained his intention finds Kirillov on the floor, surrounded by a splatter of blood and brains, a revolver still in his hand.

There are several strands in this story. One has to do with the nature of atheism, which Dostoevsky believed was a project of self-deification. Having renounced the idea of any divine power outside the human world, human beings could not avoid claiming divine powers for themselves. If they could not abolish death, they could prove themselves superior to it. That is what Kirillov imagined he was doing by killing himself. Very few were capable of such defiance. But by sacrificing themselves, they – like Christ – redeemed all of humankind.

Another strand in the novel concerns the destructive force of sacrificial projects in politics. Like Nechaev, the conspirators portrayed in the novel believe any means can be justified if they lead to freedom. The result, in their case, was squalid murder. But if their philosophy was applied on a larger scale, Dostoevsky believed, the result would be a type of tyranny more extreme and more destructive than any in the past. He puts this conclusion into the mouth of Shigalyov, the chief theorist of the group:

> ... I am suggesting my own system of world organization ... [But] my system is not finished. I got entangled in my own data, and my conclusion directly contradicts the idea from which I start. Starting from unlimited freedom, I conclude with unlimited despotism. I will add, however, that apart from my solution of the social formula, there can be no other.[24]

Other members of the group suggest that realizing Shigalyov's vision would require 'removing the will from nine tenths of mankind and remaking them into a herd, by means of a re-educating of entire generations'. Only in this way can an earthly paradise be created. But remaking humankind can advance only 'by radically lopping off a hundred million heads' – a task that might take 'fifty, or, say, thirty years' to accomplish.[25]

As a premonition of what would be the practical result of one such scheme of human emancipation – communism – the vision Dostoevsky expresses here is remarkably prescient. The casualties of the Soviet experiment ran into tens of millions, while Mao's regime is estimated to have killed around seventy million people. These statistics do not include the numberless lives that were shortened or broken.

Dostoevsky had no remedy for the ills he diagnosed. His political views were shaped by a type of Russian messianism in which a Romantic picture of the country's culture and place in the world were mixed with pan-Slavism and anti-Semitism. Aside from pogroms and ruin for Russia, nothing would come of this toxic concoction. But Dostoevsky's aim in *Demons* was not principally prophecy. It was to pursue the human rebellion against theodicy, secular or religious. This is a theme explored in many of Dostoevsky's writings, but nowhere more than in *The Brothers Karamazov*.

As it has been envisioned in Christianity, and then in humanist visions of progress to a new world, theodicy is the pursuit of harmony. Containing no tragic conflicts, a new society would be like the

Christian heaven. But Ivan Karamazov, a rationalist who cannot make sense of the world, rejects all ideals of harmony:

> ... I absolutely renounce all higher harmony. It is not worth one little tear of even that one tormented child who beat her chest with her little fist and prayed to 'dear God' in a stinking outhouse with her unredeemed tears! ... I don't want harmony, for love of mankind I don't want it. I want to remain with unrequited suffering. I'd rather remain with my unrequited suffering and my unquenched indignation, *even if I am wrong*. Besides, they put too high a price on harmony; we can't afford to pay so much for admission. And therefore I hasten to return my ticket. And it is my duty, if only as an honest man, to return it as far ahead of time as possible. Which is what I'm doing. It's not that I don't accept God, Alyosha, I just most respectfully return him the ticket.[26]

What Ivan is rejecting is not only Christian theodicy but any idea that tries to reconcile him to the evils of the world. He would be horrified by the philosophy of Spinoza, discussed in Chapter 7, in which these evils are a necessary part of the rational order of things. Ivan refuses all such consolations. Like Kirillov, he rebels against God. The French existentialist thinker Albert Camus wrote of Kirillov that 'his reasoning is classic in its clarity. If God does not exist, Kirillov is God. If God does not exist, Kirillov must kill himself. The logic is absurd, but it is what is needed.'[27] But Ivan's reasoning is not absurd in this way. His revolt is not an expression of self-will. He has no way out. He is trapped in impotent hatred of God and the world.

Whether Ivan's attitude expressed that of Dostoevsky is an intriguing question. Referring to another member of the revolutionary group, Kirillov says: 'If Stavrogin believes, he does not believe that he believes. And if he does not believe, he does not believe he does not believe.'[28] Whatever Dostoevsky believed, he could not accept that God was all good. He found difficulty in imagining any kind of goodness. As has often been noted, the 'good' characters in Dostoevsky's novels are unconvincing. This is certainly so in *The Brothers Karamazov*. Sly, cynical and selfish, Fyodor Pavlovich Karamazov is more believable than any of his three sons, though Dmitri – who murders his father – resembles him in some ways. Like many of

Dostoevsky's embodiments of virtue, Alexei Fyodorovich Kara-mazov ('Alyosha'), the youngest of the brothers and a novice in a Russian Orthodox monastery who was regarded by Dostoevsky as the hero of the novel, has something of the holy fool about him. Alyosha's teacher, the Elder Zosima, comes across as a sententious old bore. While Dostoevsky may have believed in goodness, he writes as if he did not believe that he believed.

The parable of the Grand Inquisitor shows Dostoevsky at his most paradoxical. Jesus came into the world with a promise of freedom. When he returns during the time of the Spanish Inquisition, he is soon recognized and taken into the charge of the Cardinal Grand Inquis-itor, 'an old man, almost ninety, tall and straight, with a gaunt face and sunken eyes, from which a glitter still shines like a fiery spark'.

Jesus' error, the Inquisitor tells him, was in believing that human-kind wants freedom. In fact, it has neither the capacity nor the desire to be free. What it wants is its daily bread, along with a show of mys-tery and authority. Most human beings dread freedom as the worst curse that could befall them:

Freedom, free reason, and science will lead them into such a maze, and confront them with such miracles and insoluble mysteries, that some of them, unruly and ferocious, will exterminate themselves; others, unruly but feeble, will exterminate each other; and the remain-ing third will crawl to our feet and cry out to us, 'Yes, you were right . . . and we are coming back to you – save us from ourselves' . . . And everyone will be happy, all the millions of creatures, except for the hundred thousand who govern them. For only *we*, who keep the mystery, only we shall be unhappy. There will be thousands of mil-lions of happy babes, and a hundred thousand sufferers who have taken on themselves the curse of the knowledge of good and evil. Peacefully they will die, peacefully they will expire in your name, and beyond the grave they will find only death. But we will keep the secret, and for their own happiness we will entice them with a heavenly and eternal reward . . . Tomorrow, you will see this obedient flock, which at my first gesture will heap hot coals around your stake, at which I shall burn you for having come to interfere with us. For if anyone has deserved our stake, it is you.[29]

But Jesus is not burnt at the stake. Having been silent throughout the Inquisitor's peroration, listening 'intently and calmly' and 'apparently not wanting to contradict anything', he approaches the old man and kisses him. The Inquisitor goes to the door of the prison cell, opens it and says to Jesus, 'Go and do not come again ... do not come at all ... never, never!' The prisoner goes away.

The philosophy of the Grand Inquisitor is that of the Nihilists better worked out. The heart of the parable is the Inquisitor's atheism. 'Yes, that alone is the whole secret ...' The Inquisitor is an atheist who does not love God but has somehow not lost his love of humankind.

Ivan's parable contains a number of puzzles. It has the Inquisitor following the guidance of Satan. But Satan has always been – in Christianity, at any rate – a rebel against God. How can there be any such rebellion if there is no God? After all, the Grand Inquisitor does not believe in God. Did Dostoevsky himself believe not in God but only in the Devil? The picture of Satan he presents, when towards the end of the novel Ivan suffers a brain fever and has a hallucinatory visitation, suggests otherwise.

Dostoevsky's Satan is not Milton's, a proud angel who defies God. He is a shifty, amiable, down-at-heel aristocrat: 'a certain type of Russian gentleman, no longer young ... with not too much grey in his dark, rather long and still thick hair, and with a pointed beard. He was wearing a sort of brown jacket, evidently from the best of tailors, but already shabby ... His linen, his long, scarf-like necktie, all was just what every stylish gentleman would wear, but on closer inspection, the linen was a bit dirty and the wide scarf was threadbare.' The Devil is unhappy with his task, though not unduly so. He finds his ghostly existence unnerving. What he would really like is to be incarnated, finally and irrevocably, as a human being – ideally, 'some fat, two-hundred-and-fifty pound merchant's wife, and to believe everything she believes'. When asked by Ivan if there is a God, the Devil replies, 'I just don't know.'

If the Devil has a philosophy, it is Kirillov's:

In my opinion there is no reason to destroy anything, one need only destroy the idea of God in mankind ... Man, his will and science no longer limited, conquering nature every hour, will thereby experience such lofty delight as will replace for him all his hopes of heavenly delight. Each will know himself utterly mortal, without resurrection, and will accept death proudly and calmly, like a god . . . Lovely![30]

Such a heaven on earth will never be realized, of course. But, the Devil goes on, if there is no God and no immortality, anyone who knows the truth 'is permitted to settle things for himself, absolutely as he wishes, on new principles. In this sense, "everything is permitted" to him.' Anyone who can live by this precept becomes a man-god, even if a new world never comes. But Kirillov's philosophy leaves one question unanswered: if everything is permitted, why should a god-like human being have any care for the rest of humanity? The Inquisitor believes that humankind can be cured of its unhappiness if it renounces the impulse of rebellion. His task is to ensure that this renunciation is accomplished and made secure. But why should the Inquisitor sacrifice his own happiness for the sake of humanity? Does the belief that he is redeeming humankind bring him happiness after all?

Dostoevsky answered none of these questions. But he seems to have believed in human unhappiness more than in anything else. The most penetrating of his interpreters, the Russian-Jewish religious writer Lev Shestov, whose fideist philosophy is discussed in Chapter 7, described him as 'the great artist in human misery'.[31] Aside from the epiphany he experienced when he faced the firing-squad, Dostoevsky's own life was one of almost unremitting unhappiness. He fought a long losing struggle with a gambling addiction, vividly portrayed in the novella *The Gambler* (1866), itself written to pay off debts contracted via the roulette wheel, and his wife and family suffered terribly as a result. He was chronically unhappy and spread unhappiness around him. The 'cruelty' that has been detected in his writings may have been the product of guilt-fuelled masochism.

A rejection of theodicy is the heart of Dosteovsky's work. In his conversation with Alyosha, Ivan says:

'One cannot live by rebellion, and I want to live. Tell me straight out, I call on you – answer me: imagine that you yourself are building the edifice of human destiny, with the object of making people happy in the finale, of giving them peace and rest, but that you must inevitably and unavoidably torture just one tiny creature, that same child who was beating her breast with her little fist, and raise your edifice on the foundation of her unrequited tears – would you agree to be the architect on such conditions? Tell me the truth.'

'No, I would not agree,' Alyosha said softly.[32]

The Russian writer Vasily Rozanov (for a time married to a former lover of Dostoevsky's, the writer Polina Suslova) noted in an early book-length study of the Grand Inquisitor story, published in 1891, that this passage repeats almost word for word one in Dostoevsky's *Writer's Diary*.[33] When Ivan declares that he wants to hand back his ticket, he speaks for Dostoevsky himself. Ivan wanted to be an atheist, whereas Dostoevsky wanted to be a Christian. But like his fictional creation Dostoevsky rebelled against any order in the world, whether created by God or not.

WILLIAM EMPSON: GOD AS A BELSEN COMMANDANT

'The chief thing I felt I had learned, after trying to consider ethics in a fundamental manner, is that what Christians are worshipping, with their incessant advertisements for torture, is literally the Devil.'[34] Such was the conclusion of William Empson in the chapter he devoted to Christianity in *Milton's God* (first published in 1961), one of the great books of criticism in the English language. The product of a highly original and penetrating intelligence, Empson's judgement is revealing as an expression of the confusion of the secular humanist mind.

Born in 1906, Empson had an interesting life. In 1925, after being educated at Winchester College, he won a scholarship to Magdalene College, Cambridge, where he studied mathematics and then English. He was expelled in 1929 when one of the college porters found condoms in his rooms and his name was removed from the college books. Having lost any prospect of a position in academic life, he considered becoming a journalist or a civil servant. Instead his tutor I. A. Richards encouraged him to apply for posts in East Asia, and in 1931 he took up a position in a teachers' training college in Japan. For some years he taught in China, mostly from memory owing to a lack of books, sleeping on a blackboard when his university was forced to move to Kunming during the Japanese siege of Beijing. By the late 1930s he was well regarded in London literary circles – his best-known book *Seven Types of Ambiguity*, written when he was only twenty-two, was published in 1930 and a collection of poems appeared in 1935 – but still scraping a living. During the Second World War he worked at the BBC alongside George Orwell and the poet Louis MacNeice.

Returning to China in 1947 to teach in Beijing, Empson lived through the tumultuous years just before and after Mao came to power, leaving only when the ideological demands of the regime had become intolerably repressive. He continued his academic career at Kenyon College, Ohio, and then at the University of Sheffield, where he was appointed head of the English Department in 1953 and where he remained until his retirement in 1972. He disdained academic jargon, writing in a light, glancing style. Fond of drink and bohemian in appearance – T. S. Eliot, who admired his brilliance and enjoyed his company, commented on Empson's scruffiness – he lived in a state of eccentric disorder that the poet Robert Lowell described as having 'a weird, sordid nobility'. He was actively bisexual, marrying Hetta Crouse, a free-spirited South African-born sculptor with whom he enjoyed an open relationship, sometimes turbulent but apparently never without affection.

Empson's later years were less interesting. His views on politics reflected the high-minded silliness normal among academics then and later – he continued to see Mao's regime as a liberating force long after the extreme repression it practised was unambiguously clear, for example – though he departed from intellectual orthodoxy in developing a fondness for the British monarchy. In 1979 he was knighted, and awarded an honorary fellowship by the college that half a century earlier had struck his name from the books. He died in 1984.

Though not often so strongly expressed, the misotheism by which

Empson was possessed lies behind much modern atheist thinking. He believed the Christian God to be pure evil. 'The only appropriate passion, it seems to me, is that of cold horror at the "justice" of God, as at a commandant of Belsen.'[35] In another passage he wrote that the Christian God 'is astonishingly like Uncle Joe Stalin; the same patience under an appearance of roughness, the same flashes of joviality, the same thorough unscrupulousness, the same real bad temper'. The suggestion that Stalin's chief fault was bad temper is curious, but let that pass. There can be no doubt as to how Empson regarded the Christian God: 'The Christian God the Father,' he wrote, 'the God of Tertullian, Augustine and Aquinas, is the wickedest thing yet invented by the black heart of man.'[36]

It is a dramatic assertion. But where did Empson acquire this idea of evil? He was aware of a problem: 'I recognise that my own position about ethics is too indefinite.'[37] In fact Empson's position in ethics was not so much indefinite as incoherent. He wrote: 'I am still inclined to the theory of Bentham that was in favour when I was a student at Cambridge; that the satisfaction of an impulse is in itself an elementary good, and that the practical question is merely how to satisfy the greatest number.'[38] But he acknowledged that there is 'a basic objection to the theory': 'The satisfaction of an impulse to inflict pain on another person must have its equal democratic right.' This makes it sound as if wanting to inflict pain on another person is wrong only if that other person lacks the ability to inflict a similar pain. But Empson goes on at once to say that 'this satisfaction is an elementary evil . . . a remarkable object, carrying the only inherent or metaphysical evil in the world.'

Here Empson departed from Jeremy Bentham, who believed the satisfaction derived from causing pain was in principle no less valuable than any other. The impulse to cruelty was not a 'metaphysical evil'. If it had to be curbed – as Bentham recognized it did – it was not because it was bad in itself but because it tended to reduce the total sum of satisfaction in the world. If some means could be found to gratify the impulse while removing this risk, there would be nothing wrong with cruelty. The satisfaction derived from inflicting pain was an elementary good just like any other.

In taking this position, Bentham showed how far he had travelled from Christian values. Unlike his follower John Stuart Mill, he made no attempt to distinguish between higher and lower pleasures. No pleasure – not even the pleasure of cruelty – was intrinsically bad. Bentham had no conception of evil, and in this regard he reverted to the values of the pre-Christian Greco-Roman world. There is no evidence that when they watched gladiators butcher one another in the arena Roman audiences felt they were indulging a wicked pleasure. The spectacle was entertaining enough to justify itself. The notion that cruelty is 'the only inherent or metaphysical evil in the world', which Empson and other humanists have made the basis of a secular morality, could not have occurred to them.

By invoking an idea of metaphysical evil, Empson showed he remained wedded to a Christian worldview. Greco-Roman polytheism contained mischievous gods, but no idea that the world is a site of conflict between good and evil forces. No conception of evil as an active force can be found in the Hebrew Bible, where Satan appears as a messenger of God rather than an embodiment of malevolence. The serpent in the Genesis myth is identified as satanic only in the New Testament. A problem of evil is posed in the Book of Job, but it has to do with why good people suffer and does not involve any actively malign force. Dualistic visions in which the world is a battleground of good and evil forces originate in the Persian religion of Zoroastrianism which helped shape Manicheism, the original faith of St Augustine, and thereby informed Christianity. In medieval times, dualism surfaced in movements such as Catharism, which under the influence of Gnosticism believed that the visible world was created and ruled by Satan.[39]

Within Christianity, the problem of evil is insoluble. Evangelical atheism faces a similar difficulty. If religion is evil, why is humankind so attached to it? Or is it humankind that is evil? Empson never faced up to these questions. His account of Christianity is one-sided, indeed monomaniacal. His targets were those he described as 'neo-Christians' – liberal humanists who failed to recognize how morally repugnant Christianity actually was. He failed to recognize how much he was himself a neo-Christian.

He came to his damning judgement of the Christian God by

considering the Christian heaven. God had tortured himself to death (in the person of his son) in order to redeem humankind from a condition of sinfulness; but this was a condition into which he had tricked Adam and Eve in the Garden of Eden. Worse, God had prescribed eternal torment for anyone who did not believe in this dreadful story. Worst of all, the Christian God had made believers complicit in this scheme by rewarding them with a spectacle of everlasting torment.

Empson quotes from St Thomas Aquinas: 'Nothing should be denied the blessed that belongs to the perfection of their beatitude . . . Wherefore in order that the happiness of saints may be more delightful to them and that they render more copious thanks to God for it, they are allowed to see perfectly the sufferings of the damned.'[40] The heaven that Aquinas describes resembles nothing so much as a Nazi concentration camp:

> Survivors of Nazi concentration camps agree that the most powerful technique used there for the destruction of human conscience and personality was a more subtle one than might be expected in such a brutal setting; each of the starving and tormented prisoners was tempted, by the offer of very small alleviations, to take a turn in torturing his fellows. Except that the blessed are offered no activity, this is what the Christians have to regard as Heaven . . .[41]

Once it is seen clearly, 'the Christian God becomes nakedly bad.' Why has this God constructed a cosmic system of torture? 'The only intelligible motive is a sadistic one,' Empson replies.[42] But how has such a sadistic vision managed to impose itself on so many people for so many centuries? Empson's answer is that Christianity encouraged 'mucking about with people's sex', 'a grass-roots way for Christians to gratify their God'.[43] But why should this grass-roots movement have spread so far and have lasted so long? Christians were brainwashed: ' "brain-washing" is not a new scientific invention, and Hitler had no opportunity to use "the technique of the biggest lie" as grandly as the Christians – since they worship as the source of all goodness a God who, as soon as you are told the basic story about him, is evidently the Devil.'[44] Here Empson repeats a familiar

Enlightenment accusation, according to which the errors and vices of Christianity have been imposed on humankind by the machinations of a wicked few.

Notwithstanding his reference to 'the black heart of man', Empson believed that cruelty was repugnant to the 'unspoilt taste' of human beings.[45] Kindness is the natural human condition. Sadism, he wrote, is 'a sexual perversion oddly and shockingly at home in the human psyche but rather hard to teach without interference with normal sex . . . the fires of unsatisfied sex can be relied upon to stoke the fires of Hell.'[46] The implication is that the pleasures of cruelty would not have appealed to large numbers of human beings if they had not been corrupted by Christianity.

This idea is contradicted by the example of the Aztecs, which Empson himself cites, whose way of life was founded on spectacles of human sacrifice. He writes that there is 'evidence for a certain brotherhood' between their practices and Christianity. But the Aztecs could not have acquired a taste for cruelty from Christianity, which was unknown to them until the Christian conquistadores destroyed their way of life and their religion.[47]

If you look beyond Christian and anti-Christian polemic, you do not need to invoke religion to explain cruelty. Like kindness, it goes with being human. A more interesting question is why cruelty should have come to be seen as the supreme vice – the only thing in the world, according to Empson, which is intrinsically evil. In a godless universe, how can anything be 'metaphysically evil'? Evil in the sense of malevolence assumes agency of some kind. If no such agent exists, then – as Leopardi recognized – there is no problem of evil.

Struggling with this insuperable difficulty, Empson ended up embracing something like Gnosticism. The God that ruled the world in Christianity was in truth the Devil. When Eve ate the apple in the Genesis story – in which, Empson believed, she is the true hero – she was generously accepting a promise that God had falsely made. In much the same way, it was God who set up Satan for rebellion. Empson portrays Milton's Satan with some sympathy, noting that he recoils when he 'must perform his first really wicked, that is, unkind action'.[48]

Satan knows that in obeying God he is doing evil. In a famous passage he declares:

> Evil be thou my Good . . .
>
> . . .
>
> Aye me, they little know
> How dearly I abide that boast so vain,
> Under what torments inwardly I groan:
> While they [Satan's disciples] adore me on the Throne of Hell
> With Diadem and Sceptre high advanced
> The lower still I fall, only supreme
> in misery . . .[49]

Empson's Satan is a noble rebel, condemned to revolt against a God he worships and also despises. His diabolical pride is a theatrical performance. The reality is despairing submission. And it is God that has put Satan in this desperate position. The Devil is an actor in a theatre of cruelty. The entire Christian drama is a cruel joke. But what if the idea that cruelty is the supreme evil is itself an inheritance from Christianity?

Empson recognized that religions contain conflicting strands of thinking and feeling. He explored this in a masterly volume on Buddhist art that was lost for nearly sixty years. The book began in the ancient Japanese city of Nara, where, in the spring of 1932, he was 'bowled over' by three statues, including the Kudara Kannon, a seventh-century piece in the Horyuji temple representing the Bodhisattva of Mercy. They fascinated him because the left and right profiles of the statue seemed to reveal asymmetrical expressions: 'The puzzlement and good humour of the face are all on the left, also the maternity and the rueful but amiable smile. The right is the divinity; a birdlike innocence and wakefulness; unchanging in irony, unresting in good works; not interested in humanity, or for that matter in itself . . . a wonderfully subtle and tender work.'

Enchanted by these images, Empson travelled widely in the years that followed, visiting south-east Asia, Korea, China, Ceylon, Burma and India and ending up in the caves of Ajanta, the fountainhead of Mahayana Buddhist art. *The Face of the Buddha*[50] was written in the course of these wanderings.

Empson made no copy of the manuscript, and in a series of mishaps it was lost. On leaving for foreign travels in 1947 he gave the manuscript to John Davenport, a family friend and literary critic, for safekeeping. But the hard-drinking Davenport mislaid the MS, and in 1952 told Empson he had left it in a taxi. Davenport's memory was befuddled. He had in fact given the text to the Tamil poet M. J. T. Tambimuttu, who must have shelved it among the piles of books that filled his rat-infested flat. When Tambimuttu returned to Ceylon in 1949 he passed on Empson's manuscript to Richard Marsh, a fellow editor of *Poetry London*, which Tambimuttu had founded. Marsh died soon afterwards and his papers mouldered in obscurity until 2003, when they were acquired by the British Museum. Two years later a Museum curator spotted the manuscript and told the author's descendants of its rediscovery.

Empson's interest in Buddhism runs throughout his life. While working in the Far Eastern Department of the BBC he wrote the outline of a ballet, *The Elephant and the Birds*, based on a story of the Buddha in his incarnation as an elephant found in Buddhist scriptures. His enduring fascination with the Buddha is evident in 'The Fire Sermon', a personal translation of the Buddha's famous sermon which Empson used as the epigraph in successive editions of his collected poems.[51]

Like the images of the Buddha he loved, Empson's attitude to Buddhism was asymmetrical. He valued Buddhism as an alternative to the modern western outlook in which satisfying one's desires is the principal or only goal in life. He believed that by asserting the painfulness of existence – whether earthly or heavenly – Buddhism was more life-negating and in this regard even worse than Christianity. Yet he also believed that Buddhism had in practice been more life-enhancing. Buddhism was a paradox – a seeming contradiction that contained a vital truth.

What Empson admired in Buddhist art was its ability to reconcile conflicting values. 'It may be', he wrote in *Complex Words*, 'that the human mind can recognise actually incommensurable values, and that the chief human value is to stand up between them.'[52] The image of the Buddha in Nara embodied this stance. Rather than trying to contain conflicting values in an ideal of perfection as Christianity had done, the Buddhist image fused their conflicts into a paradoxical whole. Entering into an initially alien form of art and religion, Empson found a point of balance between values and emotions whose conflicts are universal.

He was unable to see how a similar balance between conflicting values could be found in the Christian religion. Christianity invented a suffering God; a cruel vision. But by picturing God as suffering, Christianity may also have made cruelty sinful.

If the Christian universe is a vast torture-chamber, it is also a universe in which human suffering has moral significance. In the ancient world of the Greeks and Romans, suffering might be the work of the gods; but the gods were arbitrary and capricious. Christianity answered a need ancient polytheism could not satisfy: it gave misery meaning and value. By taking suffering out of the realm of blind chance, Christianity imposed a responsibility on those who inflicted it.

Empson's genius was in recognizing the irreducible plurality of meaning and value in language and art. He saw this plurality in the contradictory expressions of the Buddha. He was too close to Christianity to see it there too. Along with Nietzsche, he rejected the Christian religion because it humiliated humankind. He resented the idea that human beings are in need of redemption: 'Terms such as "redemption", deep into human experience though they undoubtedly plunge,' he wrote severely, 'are metaphors drawn from the slave market.'[53] In other words, Christianity denied human freedom. But the freedom Empson invoked against Christianity was a Jewish and Christian creation. As the Russian Orthodox writer Nikolai Berdyaev observed: 'The idea of the Fall is at bottom a proud idea, and through it man escapes from the sense of humiliation. If man fell away from God he must have been an exalted creature, endowed with great freedom and power.'[54]

Empson was a neo-Christian to the end. Only someone as steeped in Christianity as Milton could have imagined the Devil as a noble figure. In taking the Devil's side, Empson was re-enacting a Christian drama.

6

Atheism without Progress

GEORGE SANTAYANA, AN ATHEIST WHO LOVED RELIGION

Recounting a conversation he had with George Santayana when he visited the aged philosopher in Rome, the American novelist and essayist Gore Vidal recalled how disconcerted he had been by Santayana's mischievous detachment from the human world:

> Even at eighty-five the clear black eyes shone as bright and as hard as obsidian. When I said to him with youthful despair that the world had never yet been in so terrible a state Santayana could not have been more brisk, or chilling. 'My own life-time has been spent in a longer period of peace and security than that of almost anyone I could conceive of in the European past.' When I spoke with horror and revulsion of the possibility that Italy ... Bella Italia ... might go communist in the next month's election, Santayana looked positively gleeful. 'Oh let them! Let them try it! They've tried everything else so why not communism. After all who knows what new loyalties will emerge as they become part of a wolf-pack?' I was sickened and revolted by his sang-froid, his cynicism.[1]

Coming from an admirer of Santayana and someone not easily shocked, it is a remarkable confession. But no one who had read Santayana with any care could be surprised by his attitude to the events of his day. One of very few philosophers to have lived in accordance with his avowed ideal of the good life, Santayana followed the ancient sages Epicurus and Lucretius in seeking a distance from the world. The pursuit of equanimity seems to have been a dominant passion throughout his life.

Born in Madrid in 1863 and spending his early years in the Spanish city of Avila, Santayana was educated in Boston after his mother and father moved to the United States. He graduated from Harvard and taught there for over twenty years, attracting students such as T. S. Eliot and Gertrude Stein and acquiring friends and admirers such as the poet Wallace Stevens. His contemporaries in the Department of Philosophy included William James, a hostile critic who described Santayana's philosophy as 'the perfection of rottenness'.

Santayana never considered academic philosophy his vocation. After receiving a small legacy he left Harvard and the United States in 1912, five years after had had been made a full professor, to live as a wandering scholar in Europe. Despite many enticements, he never returned to Harvard or to America. He gave an indication of his opinion of academic philosophers when on his resignation he followed a Harvard convention in donating books to the Department. Written by his colleagues, they were printed in this period with uncut pages. When Santayana returned them none of the pages had been cut open. None of the books had been read. Santayana's message was obvious. In the forty years that followed his departure his writings were deliberately unacademic in style: polished and glittering, studded with aphorisms, addressing the unprofessional reader in conversational terms without giving away anything of the author's life or emotions.

Santayana was uncompromising in leading the kind of life he wanted. Among academic institutions he was happiest at Oxford, where he lived for the duration of the First World War. Yet he declined an offer of a permanent fellowship at Corpus Christi College arranged by the poet Robert Bridges, though the post would not have involved any teaching or administrative duties. He feared that being confined in an academic institution would have limited his freedom of mind. This need for independence also dictated the terms of his personal life. He has been described as a gay celibate, and while we cannot know how strict or otherwise his celibacy may have been he never acquired a partner. His biographer John McCormick cites a passage in which he celebrates sexual passion: 'Frank love is not in the least distracting; it is hearty, joyful, and gay; or if any mood follows in which it is viewed at a certain remove, as an odd performance, it still leaves an after-glow of laughter and affection.' McCormick comments: 'This, surely, is the philosophy of a lover, not a virginal celibate.'[2] But there is no evidence that Santayana allowed himself to fall in love. He may have made a conscious decision to renounce the experience for the sake of peace of mind. In doing so, he would have acknowledged a cost in happiness. In a late auto-biographical passage, he wrote:

> Spirit is an emanation of life, and is more truly and naturally happy in the first phases of its career than in its final salvation. In the end, when it has understood and renounced everything, it can reply only as La Vallière replied to the friends who asked her if she were happy in the Carmelite convent to which she had retired: *Je ne suis pas heureuse: je suis content* [I am not happy: I am content].[3]

Louise de La Vallière (1644–1710), former mistress of Louis XIV, found tranquillity in later life by retreating to a nunnery. Santayana may have known this contentment in the Convent of the Blue Nuns, a nursing home in Rome run by the Little Company of Mary (known as the Blue Nuns because of the colour of their habits) and the place where he chose to pass the final years of his long life. He lived in the convent from 1941 until his death in September 1952.

Parsimonious in Harvard, he led a life of stylish affluence after he moved to Europe. Dressed by a first-rate tailor and jaunty in manner, he enjoyed good company, fine meals and opulent surroundings. He gave all this up for the sake of peace and quiet. He received the guests that came to see him – too often, he may have felt – in pyjamas and a frayed dressing-gown. 'The bed, the books, the chair, the moving nuns' – as Wallace Stevens pictured the life of his friend in his poem 'To an Old Philosopher in Rome' – were enough for him.

Santayana had become financially secure as a result of a novel he had written, *The Last Puritan* (1935), an American best-seller. He gave away much of the money, including a substantial anonymous donation to Bertrand Russell, whom he described as 'a leading mathematician, philosopher, militant pacifist, wit and martyr, but unfortunately addicted to marrying and divorcing not wisely but too often'.[4] In his will he left legacies to family members and the young American Daniel Cory who had acted as his assistant for many years and became his literary executor, but nothing to the Blue Nuns. When asked, two days before he died, whether he was in pain, he replied, 'Yes, my friend. But my anguish is entirely physical; there are no moral difficulties whatsoever.'[5]

Aside from a firm request that his ashes were not to be returned to the United States, Santayana left no instructions regarding the disposal of his remains, so there was a question as to where this unyielding atheist would be buried. In the end, since he had always retained his Spanish citizenship, the Consulate in Rome arranged for him to be interred in a tomb reserved for Spaniards in the Campo Verano Cemetery.

There was no hint of belief in Santayana's life in the convent. 'My atheism, like that of Spinoza,' he wrote, 'is true piety to the universe and denies only gods fashioned by men in their own image, to be servants of their human interests.'[6] In comparing himself with the seventeenth-century Jewish philosopher Benedict Spinoza, who will be discussed in the next chapter, Santayana was invoking a thinker he admired greatly. Spinoza viewed revealed religion as the work of the human imagination, just as Santayana did. But, like Santayana, he believed it contained truth that could not be conveyed in any other way.

Santayana professed himself a disciple of Lucretius. But it was Lucretius' materialism he admired, not the Roman poet's rejection of religion. Epicurean spirituality, Santayana wrote, was 'fumbling, timid and sad'. He thought Epicurus was too concerned with the avoidance of pain and extended this criticism to Epicurus' most famous disciple: 'Lucretius' notion of what is positively worthwhile or attainable is very meagre: freedom from superstition, with so much natural science as may secure that freedom, friendship, and a few cheap and healthful animal pleasures. No love, no patriotism, no enterprise, no religion.'[7]

Denying that any order that could be found in the world was the work of a divine creator, Santayana followed Lucretius in thinking that Nature is self-sufficient and often described himself as a materialist. But Santayana's materialism is very different from that of the French materialists discussed in the last chapter, who advocated returning to a benign Nature, and from that of the Marquis de Sade, who asserted that Nature was destructive and evil. For Santayana Nature is the creative energy that produces everything in the world, including the human species and all its works. Art and science, ethics and politics are natural to humans, and so is religion. In a chapter headed 'Whether Naturalism is Irreligious' in his last book, *Dominations and Powers* (1950), he wrote:

> The question is debatable because words in current use have many meanings. Thus naturalism for a pagan is far from atheistic, since it finds room for many gods. Jews and Christians were called atheists, for not worshipping the gods recognised by the State . . . The Hindus are polytheists, monotheists and pantheists at once; and the Buddhists, though technically atheists, and denying the existence of souls, are ideally so religious and spiritual that it seems grotesque for a modern Christian to tax them with atheism . . . Is it love of man that prompts hatred of religion? No, it is insensibility to the plight of man and all that which man most deeply loves.[8]

Santayana's objection to modern naturalism was that it is implicitly misanthropic: 'Why should we be angry with dreams, with myth, with allegory, with madness? We must not kill the mind, as some rationalists do, in trying to cure it.'[9] It is a strange sort of naturalism that singles out religion to be purged from human life. Few things are more natural for humans than religion.

To be sure, religion has brought much suffering. So has love and the pursuit of knowledge. Like them, religion is part of being human. But no one religion suits everyone. Any claim to prescribe a universal way of life is misguided. Towards the end of *Dominations and Powers*, Santayana made this point with particular force:

> Many philosophers and politicians indeed tell us that they already possess *a priori* an adequate knowledge of what human needs and

capacities are, and that they are really identical in everybody. The contrasts and conflicts in society, and in each man, they attribute to the absence or perversity of education. All men, they say, *must* find the same moral, political and scientific regimen, communism, or constitutional democracy, or the One True Religion perfectly satisfying. If they hesitate or condemn all such regimens, it *must* be because they are ignorant of the facts and of their own true good.

I think these philosophers and politicians have good knowledge of themselves. They are born dogmatists and congenitally militant. But this disposition of theirs, at once intolerant and uneasy, blinds them to the actual radical diversity among men ... They say we are all super-animals, either fallen from heaven or about to make a heaven for ourselves on earth.[10]

Santayana dismissed any idea that civilization was improving. Insofar as it was real, progress meant refining particular ways of living: 'The reader must not expect me to trace the fortunes of liberty historically or eschatologically, as if all were progress towards perfection. Everything in this world, considered temporally, is a progress towards death. True progress is an approach, in favourable seasons, to perfection in some kind of life.'[11] The idea that the universe is a hierarchy with God or humanity at the top Santayana repudiated entirely. Continuing progress is possible only in technology and the mechanical arts. Progress in this sense may well accelerate while the quality of civilization declines:

We all feel at this time the moral ambiguity of mechanical progress. It seems to multiply opportunity, but it destroys the possibility of simple, rural or independent life. It lavishes information, but it abolishes mastery except in trivial or mechanical proficiency. We learn many languages, but degrade our own. Our philosophy is highly critical and thinks itself enlightened, but is a Babel of mutually unintelligible artificial tongues.[12]

Santayana's view of religion follows from his criticism of progress. Religion is natural for the human animal, but not any one kind of religion. He deplored monotheism when it was militant and evangelical. The cardinal error of Christianity came from Platonism, which (for Christians who adopted it) conceived the Good to be a power in the world. Having identified itself with this power, the Church inevitably became repressive of human variety.

Platonism, and then Christianity, encouraged an illusion regarding the nature of value. For Santayana, values were animal needs turned into abstract categories and projected into the cosmos. Often condemned as a relativist, he did not blush at the description. 'Value is something relative,' he wrote, 'a dignity which anything may acquire in view of the benefit or satisfaction which it brings to some living thing.'[13]

That does not mean human values are matters of opinion. Though they are relative in that they reflect human needs and circumstances, judgements of value often stray from underlying realities. 'The good is by no means relative to opinion, but is rooted in the unconscious and fatal nature of living beings, a nature which predetermines for them the difference between foods and poisons, happiness and misery.' To this extent, there can be error in ethics. But values cannot be objective if that means being independent of living organisms: 'Values presuppose living beings having a direction of development, and exerting themselves in it, so that good and evil may exist in reference to them. That the good should be relative to actual natures and simply their innate ideal, latent or realized, is essential to its being truly a good.'[14] Without valuing organisms, there are no values. Santayana deployed this argument in a devastating critique of Bertrand Russell, who for many years was attracted to Platonism in ethics – the idea that values subsist in some ideal immaterial realm. To Russell's enormous credit, he accepted Santayana's criticisms and abandoned the Platonism he had for so long cherished.[15]

In combining a subjective view of value with an ideal of contemplation, Santayana was unusual. Nearly all of those who have valued contemplation have done so because they believed (like Plato and the early Russell) in a higher reality to which contemplation gives access. Santayana had no such belief. He valued contemplation because it enabled a lucid vision of the only world that exists – the world of matter.

Anyone who contemplates this world, Santayana suggested,

encounters 'essences' – sensations not unlike those that the narrator of Marcel Proust's novel *Remembrance of Things Past* finds springing from memory. Drinking tea in which he had soaked a morsel of cake, Proust's narrator found 'a delicious pleasure had invaded my senses, something isolated, detached, with no suggestion of its origin. And at once the vicissitudes of life had become indifferent to me, its disasters innocuous, its brevity illusory . . . I had ceased now to feel mediocre, contingent, mortal.'[16]

Santayana seems to have had a similar experience:

> a mind enlightened by scepticism and cured of noisy dogma, a mind discounting all reports and freed from all tormenting anxiety about its own fortunes and existence, finds in the wilderness of essence a very sweet and marvellous solitude. The ultimate reaches of doubt and renunciation open out for it, by an easy transition, into fields of endless variety and peace, as if through the gorges of death it had passed into a paradise where all things are crystallised into the image of themselves, and have lost their urgency and their venom.[17]

There is no suggestion here that essences exist in any higher realm. They are momentary sensations in individual minds, themselves moments in the transformations of matter.

As he recognized, Santayana's philosophy resembled the classical Hindu school of Samkhya more than any western doctrine.[18] Samkhya is distinctive in Indian thought in that it regards matter as real and independent of any mind, not an illusion created by a world-spirit. But Santayana's materialism was more far-reaching. Spirit was a flash in the dark, a transient awareness flaring up in matter itself, not a separate metaphysical reality.

Santayana shared with the Samkhya school the view that, rather than dissolving into any super-soul or world-spirit, the liberated mind would be a perfectly integrated whole. Describing this condition, Santayana sounded a Gnostic note. As the mind withdraws into itself, 'the whole natural world will be removed to a distance. It will have become foreign. It will touch us, and exist morally for us, only as the scene of our strange exile, and as being the darkness, the cravings, the confusion in which the spirit finds itself plunged, and from which, with infinite difficulty and uncertainty, it hopes to be delivered.'[19]

Whether Santayana thought any such deliverance was possible, except as a passing sensation, is doubtful. He realized that the detachment he cherished could be destroyed at any moment by the frailty of the body. He pursued it anyway: 'for after life is done, and the world is gone up in smoke, what realities may the spirit of a man boast to have embraced without illusion, save the very forms of the illusions by which he has been deceived?'[20]

The life of the spirit came not as an otherworldly mystical rapture but from disillusion with the world. But disillusion proved liberating, since it allowed a view of the world from a perspective that did not expect salvation in history: 'The world is not respectable; it is mortal, tormented, confused, deluded for ever; but it is shot through with beauty, with love, with glints of courage and laughter; and in these the spirit blooms timidly, and struggles to the light among the thorns. Such is the flitting life of this winged thing, spirit, in this old, sordid, maternal earth.'[21]

Santayana found freedom in the godless flux of matter from which mystics have struggled to escape. An ideal realm modelled on human values was no place in which to look for spiritual freedom: 'In the end such a universe, floating like a bubble in the flux of things, would almost certainly dissolve. It is not there that an enlightened heart would lay up its treasure. The flood itself is a nobler companion, and the spirit moves at ease upon the waters.'[22]

JOSEPH CONRAD AND THE GODLESS SEA

Joseph Conrad often claimed that he became a writer by chance, and the pattern of events supports his assertion. But an inner necessity was at work as well. More than any other single factor, it was his experiences in the Congo that impelled him to become an author. They left him partly broken, a semi-invalid prone to bouts of depression throughout the rest of his life. But they also made him the writer he came to be.

When asked what had led him to become a writer, he is said to have been silent for some minutes, then to have responded, 'Well, I was a long time on shore.'[23] There was some truth in this reply. When he took up writing as a career in 1894 conditions were changing in the merchant marine. Sailing ships, which he preferred over steamers, were declining in number and those that remained were not in the best condition. Crews in steamers were smaller and better paid, while the numbers of master seamen competing for positions had risen. The skills Conrad had learnt in over twenty years as a seaman were fast becoming obsolete. In any case his attitude to his vocation was ambivalent. Ford Madox Ford, who knew him well and collaborated with him as an author, went so far as to say that Conrad hated life at sea.[24]

Life in the merchant marine was hard. Living quarters were cramped and unhealthy and the food awful. Working conditions were hazardous. Conrad was injured on several occasions and survived the wreck of one ship in an open boat. On top of these dangers and privations, employment was irregular. During his twenty years as a seaman Conrad tried unsuccessfully to achieve financial independence through a series of speculative ventures, including whaling, piloting in the Suez Canal, Australian pearl fisheries, Canadian railroads and working for the Japanese navy. At the time he took up writing he was beginning to suffer from crippling gout. He could not have carried on as a seaman.

Born in 1857 into an aristocratic Polish family in Tsarist-ruled Ukraine, he spent his childhood in the Russian provinces after his father had been exiled for anti-Russian activities. Against family advice he left for France to become a cabin boy, eventually qualifying as a master mariner in 1886. Along the way he was involved in gunrunning in Spain and joined in an attempted coup by a Catholic group that aimed to establish a claim to the Spanish throne. After six months in the Congo commanding a river vessel, he never returned to the sea.

When he finally quit seafaring life he had been writing for some years, working on what would become his first novel, *Almayer's Folly*, begun in 1889 and published in 1895. He wrote in English, his third language (the others being Polish and French). He was a foreigner in England, and though it was a country he loved he always remained an alien in it. As he put it in a letter to a Polish friend, 'Homo duplex has in my case more than one meaning.'[25]

Less well known than *Heart of Darkness* but no less powerful a story about the Congo, 'An Outpost of Progress' mocks the conceit of European colonialists who imagined they were bringing freedom to savages:

> Few men realize that their life, the very essence of their character, their capabilities and their audacities, are only the expression of their belief in the safety of their surroundings. The courage, the composure, the confidence; the emotions and principles; every great and insignificant thought belongs not to the individual but to the crowd . . . But the contact with pure unmitigated savagery, with primitive nature and primitive man, brings sudden and profound trouble into the heart.[26]

Conrad suffered this trouble in the Congo, when he was confronted with the savagery of a crusade for civilization. He had a sense of being alone for the rest of his days. The task he took up as a writer was of communicating what he had seen to his civilized readers. He doubted whether he could make a living from his new vocation – a suspicion that proved correct, since though at times he made large sums he was often deep in debt. He endured regular attacks of writer's block and often despaired of ever writing again.

Conrad was supported through these trials by his devoted wife Jesse. But he seems to have needed more than family life could provide, and in 1916–17 he had an affair with the American journalist Jane Anderson.[27] A swashbuckling beauty well known in London high society, Anderson went on to marry a Spanish aristocrat, report on the Spanish Civil War from the Falangist side, spy for Italy and Japan and broadcast for the Nazis. Arrested by the American military authorities in Austria at the end of the war, she was charged with treason only to be released, and she then vanished. She is believed in later years to have lived in Spain, though the place and time of her death are unknown. Anderson was the model for Dona Rita, the heroine in Conrad's novel *The Arrow of Gold* (1919).

Conrad's last years were dogged by bad health and money troubles. When he received an official-looking letter in May 1924, he assumed it was a demand for unpaid taxes. It was an offer of a knighthood, which Conrad declined. When he died of heart failure in August of that year, he was given a Catholic funeral despite his often expressed hostility to the Christian religion. The ceremony took place during a cricket festival, and the event passed almost unnoticed. Lines from Edmund Spenser's sixteenth-century poem *The Faerie Queene*, which Conrad had used as the epigraph of his last novel *The Rover* (1923), were carved on his gravestone in Canterbury cemetery:

> Sleep after toyle, port after stormie seas,
> Ease after warre, death after life, does greatly please.

'Before the Congo, I was just a mere animal.'[28] At the time Conrad travelled in the region, the Congo was not a colony of the Belgian state but a personal fiefdom of King Leopold. At an international conference in Brussels in 1876, Leopold described his goal: 'To open to civilization the only area of our globe to which it has not yet penetrated, to pierce the gloom which hangs over entire races, constitutes, if I may dare put it in this way, a Crusade worthy of this century of Progress.'[29] In fact the territory was exploited with extraordinary brutality and its human population used as an expendable resource. As Conrad recorded in a diary of his time in the Congo, dead bodies and human bones lay around unburied. Chained slave gangs had their hands beaten with rifle butts and amputated as a punishment. When no longer useful, workers were lined up behind one another and shot with a single bullet. Sick or wounded labourers were thrown to dogs to be eaten. It is not clear how much of this Conrad himself witnessed. But what he saw was enough to affect him for the rest of his life.

Conrad's reaction to the Congo has been seen as a rejection of a Victorian idea of progress. He had seen too much of how colonialism worked in practice to believe it to be essentially civilizing. But his resistance to the idea of progress went beyond rejecting the particular vision of human improvement that Leopold and those who acted on his behalf invoked to justify their rapacity.

Conrad could not take seriously any vision of the future that involved a transformation in human nature. He expressed his incredulity in many of his letters, including some to Bertrand Russell. Seeing the chaos in China, Russell looked for a solution in 'international socialism'. Conrad's response was caustic and definitive. Russell's vision of a socialist future was:

> the sort of thing to which I cannot attach any sort of definite meaning. I have never been able to find in any man's book or any man's talk anything to stand up for a moment against my deep-seated sense of fatality governing this man-inhabited world. After all it is but a system, not very recondite and not very plausible. As a mere reverie it is not of a very high order . . . But I know you wouldn't expect me to put faith in *any* system. The only remedy for Chinamen and for the rest of us is the change of hearts, but looking at the history of the last 2000 years there is not much reason to expect that, even if man has taken to flying – a great 'uplift', no doubt, but no great change. He doesn't fly like an eagle; he flies like a beetle. And you must have noticed how ugly, ridiculous and fatuous is the flight of a beetle.[30]

In a letter to his friend R. B. Cunninghame Graham, a Scottish adventurer and socialist, Conrad wrote: 'Man is a wicked animal. His wickedness has to be organised . . . Society is essentially criminal – otherwise it would not exist.'[31]

Conrad's unsparing view of society owed little to a Christian idea of original sin. Throughout his life he found the Christian religion distasteful – 'an absurd oriental fable'.[32] In the Author's Note to *The Shadow Line*, he stated his rejection of religion in categorical terms: ' . . . I am too firm in my consciousness of the marvellous to be ever fascinated by the mere supernatural, which (take it any way you like) is but a manufactured article, the fabrication of minds insensitive to the intimate delicacies of our relation to the dead and to the living . . .'[33]

For Conrad, human beings were parts of the natural world. He did not view consciousness as an unmixed blessing. 'Thinking is the great enemy of perfection. The habit of profound reflection, I am compelled to say, is the most pernicious of all the habits formed by the civilised man.'[34] Writing again to Cunninghame Graham, he described humans as conscious beings trapped in a mechanical cosmos:

> There is a – let us say – a machine. It evolved itself (I am severely scientific) out of a chaos of scraps of iron and behold! – it knits. I am horrified at the horrible work and stand appalled. I feel it ought to embroider – but it goes on knitting ... And the most withering thought is that the infamous thing has made itself; made itself without thought, without conscience, without foresight, without heart. It is a tragic accident ... It knits us in and it knits us out. It has knitted time, space, pain, death, corruption, despair and all the illusions – and nothing matters. I'll admit however that to look at the remorseless process is sometimes amusing.[35]

Later he wrote:

> The machine is thinner than air and as evanescent as a flash of lightning ... The ardour for reform, improvement, for virtue, for knowledge, and even for beauty is only a vain sticking up for appearances ... Life knows us not and we do not know life – we don't even know our own thoughts ... Faith is a myth and belief shifts like mists on the shore.[36]

Far from consciousness being humanity's crowning glory, as humanists in his day and ours have proclaimed, it is self-awareness that makes the human predicament intractable:

> Systems could be built, and rules could be made – if we could only get rid of consciousness. What makes mankind tragic is not that they are victims of nature, it is that they are conscious of it. To be part of the animal kingdom under the conditions of the earth is very well – but as soon as you know of your slavery, the pain, the anger, the strife – the tragedy begins.[37]

Conrad explored this tragedy in *Victory* (1915), the greatest of his later novels. With consummate irony, he makes the chief protagonist the wandering son of a world-weary Swedish aristocrat, a disciple of Schopenhauer, whose version of atheism will be discussed in the next chapter (and by whose writings Conrad himself had been much influenced). Schopenhauer believed that since life is full of pain and sorrow the best course was detachment. By separating oneself from the human world and refusing any close personal bonds, the suffering of life could be kept at bay.

Influenced by this philosophy, Axel Heyst settles on the life of a drifter and ends up living in the company of a Chinese servant on an island in the Malay Archipelago. Heyst's life is disrupted when he encounters Lena, an unhappy young Englishwoman working in the orchestra of a Java hotel. Feeling pity for her, as well as desire, Heyst helps her escape and they live together on his island. Heyst's life is again disrupted when a gang of bandits lands, intending to steal treasure he is rumoured to have amassed. Realizing Lena is in danger, Heyst helps her hide in a bungalow. But one of the gang finds her there, and she is shot and fatally wounded. Heyst arrives on the scene, and Lena hands him a knife with which to defend himself. As she is dying she asks for an expression of his commitment to her. In an 'infernal mistrust of all life'[38] Heyst is unable to give it, but Lena dies believing she had saved the life of one who loved her. In despair, Heyst sets fire to the bungalow and is found dead next to her body. The story ends with a sea captain who had known Heyst saying: 'There was nothing to be done there ... Nothing!' In concluding Heyst's story in this way, Conrad may well have been echoing the closing lines of Schopenhauer's major work:

> we freely acknowledge that what remains after the complete abolition of the will is, for all who are still full of the will, assuredly nothing. But also conversely, to those in whom the will has turned and denied itself, this very real world of ours with all its suns and galaxies, is – nothing.[39]

Conrad has often been described as a sceptic. But his scepticism was not that of philosophers who question the possibility of knowledge. What Conrad questioned was the *value* of knowledge. As has been seen, he believed consciousness was of dubious worth. He shared this suspicion with Bertrand Russell, who in his secret adolescent journal wrote in 1888: 'I do wish I believed in the life eternal, for it makes me miserable to think man is merely a kind of machine endowed, unhappily for him, with consciousness.'[40] The idea that humans are 'conscious automata' had been floated in 1874 in a lecture by T. H. Huxley, whose views on evolution and ethics were discussed in Chapter 3.

When he doubted the value of consciousness, Conrad was pursuing an idea that was in the air. It is what he did with the question that is striking. In the character of Heyst, Conrad asks if illusion might not be more humanly worthwhile than a heightened self-awareness that denudes life of meaning. Any prospect of a worthwhile life without illusions might itself be an illusion.

Long before he wrote *Victory*, Conrad had pursued these questions in the character of Singleton in *The Nigger of the Narcissus* (1897). The first of Conrad's 'English' novels in that it is not set in the Far East, the book has not much in the way of incident. Recounting the homeward voyage of the *Narcissus* from Bombay to London, the narrator describes how the crew deals with the hazards of the journey, which include the ship being flooded when it toppled on one side in stormy seas off the Cape of Good Hope. The characters include James Wait, a black sailor from St Kitts and the 'nigger' of the title, Donkin, a roguish Cockney seaman, and Singleton, 'a lonely relic of a devoured and forgotten generation'.

The action centres round Wait, pictured as an ailing man who first attracts sympathy from the rest of the crew but comes to be seen as a tyrannical malingerer. Superstitiously, Singleton foretells that Wait will die at the sight of land. Singleton's prophecy proves correct, and Wait's death weakens the solidarity of the group. When the *Narcissus* arrives home and is towed up the Thames, they leave the freedom of the sea behind and go their separate ways.

The novel has been read as Conrad's affirmation of human solidarity, and it is true that the book pays homage to the virtues he found in the shipmates with whom he shared his life at sea. But another meaning is intimated in a letter to Cunninghame Graham, which Conrad wrote after his friend had suggested that Singleton might have been more credible if he had been equipped with an education. Conrad replied:

You say: 'Singleton with an education' . . . But first of all – what education? If it is the knowledge of how to live my man essentially possessed it. He was in perfect accord with his life. If by education you mean scientific knowledge then the question arises – what knowledge, how much of it – in what direction? Is it to stop at plane trigonometry or at conic sections? Or is he to study Platonism or Pyrrhonism or the philosophy of the gentle Emerson? Or do you mean the kind of knowledge that would enable him to scheme, and lie, and intrigue his way to the forefront of a crowd no better than himself? Would you seriously, of malice prepense cultivate in that unconscious man the power to think? Then he would become conscious – and much smaller – and very unhappy. Now he is simple and great like an elemental force. Nothing can touch him but the curse of decay – the eternal decree that will extinguish the sun, the stars one by one, and in another instant shall spread a frozen darkness over the whole universe. Nothing else can touch him – he does not think.

Would you seriously wish to tell such a man: 'Know thyself.' Understand thou art nothing, less than a shadow, more insignificant than a drop of water in the ocean, more fleeting than the illusion of a dream. Would you?[41]

It is a devastating criticism of rationalism in ethics. Since Socrates it has been assumed that an examined life will be a good life. Conrad rejects this faith. If you examine yourself, you may find that your habitual responses to life melt away. Rationalists welcome this as an opportunity to choose their path in life. They imagine that the right way of living can be found by the use of reason. But that is because they inherit a belief that the world is rational – the faith of Plato, Christianity and secular humanism. If there is no order at the bottom of things, an examined life may hardly be worth living.

In contrast, Singleton knows how to live. He has a code that shapes his actions. It has been made by human beings, but not made by him or any single generation. It is a way of life he found among his shipmates, which he refined in the course of his encounter with the sea.

The sea's indifference is not regarded by Singleton or his shipmates with any resentment. As Conrad's narrator writes: 'On men reprieved by its disdainful mercy, the immortal sea confers in its justice the full privilege of desired unrest. Through the perfect wisdom of its grace they are not permitted to meditate at ease upon the complicated and acrid savour of existence.'[42] Singleton was not blessed by any saving faith that Conrad lacked. Instead, he had the self-possession that comes from being able to assert oneself, without much thought, in situations that cannot be remedied. This capacity to face up to fate defined Conrad's rejection of the idea of progress and his atheism.

The seamen's struggle with the ocean is a cipher for the human situation in a godless universe. Conrad found the mechanical process in which humans are caught tragic. None of the visions of improvement conjured up by modern thinkers could stand up against his 'deep-seated sense of fatality governing this man-inhabited world'. But it was this invincible fatality that evoked the qualities he found most worthwhile in human beings.

Conrad did not mourn the passing of a God through which human personality was projected throughout the universe. It was the impersonality of the sea – 'the perfect wisdom of its grace', as he put it in what must surely have been an ironical theological allusion – that gave human beings their freedom. The godless ocean gave Conrad's seamen all they needed, and Conrad everything he wanted.

7

The Atheism of Silence

THE MYSTICAL ATHEISM OF
ARTHUR SCHOPENHAUER

If Nietzsche shouted the death of God from the rooftops, Arthur Schopenhauer gave the Deity a quiet burial. He showed no sign of mourning God's passing. Far more than his wayward disciple ever could, he left monotheism behind him without regret. Schopenhauer was born in the city of Danzig in 1788. His father was a man of strong will who nevertheless suffered from anxiety attacks and seems to have committed suicide, his mother a woman of high intelligence who authored some interesting novels and created an influential salon. Brought up in a household that was Christian by the conventional standards of the day, he seems never to have imbibed anything of Christian piety. If Schopenhauer had a religion in his youth, or at any time in his life, it was music.

It was in music that he found intimations of a realm beyond the human world. The nature of things, he came to think, was ineffable. Language could not capture the reality that lay behind changing appearances. But what could not be spoken could still be sung or played. What music hinted at was not the God of Christian belief. It was more like the God of negative theologians – a state of pure being. In order for this God to show itself, the Christian God had to be given the last rites and put to rest.

Himself extremely wilful, Schopenhauer was convinced that all human troubles came from the will – the restless, insatiable craving that impelled everything that existed. Anyone who grasped this truth would turn away from life and mortify their appetites, he believed.

Schopenhauer did nothing of the kind. Once he had achieved financial independence, he lived exactly as he pleased.

He followed a daily routine, writing in the morning, then walking one of the succession of poodles he kept throughout his life, playing the flute and attending the opera, enjoying good food and an occasional draught of wine. Never marrying, he pursued erotic pleasure wherever he could enjoy it without curbing his independence. A sexual diary he kept was burnt after his death, but we know from his published writings that he considered sex the dominant human impulse, more powerful than self-preservation and more pervasive than motiveless cruelty, which like Dostoevsky he recognized as a formative human impulse. Schopenhauer's reflections on 'The metaphysics of sexual love' in *The World as Will and Representation* had a deep impact on Sigmund Freud.

Believing most human beings to be incurably irrational, Schopenhauer managed his life with exceptional prudence. He may have found the human world a vale of suffering but he took care not to suffer much himself. Ideally, he favoured self-renunciation. In practice, he lived by the maxims of bourgeois wisdom. Unlike Nietzsche, there was nothing in Schopenhauer of the saint – and he knew it. He summarized the practical wisdom by which he lived in a number of essays, which collected together were published in many editions and languages.[1]

In the event Schopenhauer led a double existence, carefully cultivating his pleasures while endlessly preaching the futility of desire. For anyone who believes that philosophers must live by their teachings – as Santayana did, for example – this may look like hypocrisy. But in some ways it was a life of creative contradiction. Schopenhauer's prudent self-management enabled him to produce some of the most penetrating and best-written texts in modern philosophy. Nor was his selfishness altogether unappealing. For anyone weary of self-admiring world-improvers, there is something refreshing in Schopenhauer's nastiness.

The way of life he crafted for himself was one of disciplined intellectual labour, carefully managed hedonism and regular release through music. Fond of his pleasures, he was also anxious about his health. He was careful with money. Having received an inheritance from his father's business, he cherished his private income as an indispensable condition of his freedom – and not only from the need to engage in menial labour as a shipping clerk, which he had done for two years and feared would be his lifelong fate. Private wealth also freed him from the need to write for a living. He was relieved from any need to appease publishers or to submit himself to the judgement of his contemporaries in philosophy, whom he ridiculed and despised.

For Schopenhauer's unruly disciple Nietzsche, son of a pastor, the death of God was the greatest event in history – a rupture from which a new meaning would have to be willed into being if humankind was not to fall into an abyss of nihilism. For Schopenhauer history never did have any meaning, and no act of will could give sense to the drift of human events. For anyone reared in Christian hopes, this would mean despair. That was because they still looked to history for redemption. But, if they could shed these false hopes, they would find that lack of meaning in history was itself redemptive – a stimulus to renouncing the world. As Schopenhauer put it in a biting essay against Christianity:

> A religion which has as its foundation a *single event*, and in fact tries to make the turning-point of the world and of all existence out of that event that occurred at a definite time and place, has so feeble a foundation that it cannot possibly survive . . . How wise in *Buddhism*, on the other hand, is the assumption of the thousand Buddhas . . . The many Buddhas are necessary because at the end of each *kalpa* [cosmic epoch] the world perishes, and with it the teaching, so that a new world requires a new Buddha. Salvation always exists.[2]

Rejecting Christianity, Schopenhauer also rejected any philosophy in which history is a process of human self-emancipation. 'What history relates', he wrote, 'is in fact only the long, heavy and confused dream of mankind.' He dismissed with contempt the philosophy of G. W. F. Hegel, the foremost German thinker of the age, according to which history was the progressive unfoldment of a world-spirit – a view Schopenhauer rightly believed was Christian theodicy in disguise.

Schopenhauer detested Hegel. During a brief period of university teaching in Berlin, he provocatively scheduled his lectures at exactly the same time as those of the great man. But only a handful of students gathered to hear Schopenhauer discourse on 'the essence of the world and of the human spirit', whereas over 200 flocked to hear Hegel expatiate on the inner logic of history. Hegel demonstrated, to his own satisfaction and presumably that of his audience, that history was rational and also gratifyingly moral. It was history's inner logic that had produced the magnificent Prussian state. For Schopenhauer this was just the assertion that 'might is right' dressed up in metaphysical verbiage.

Schopenhauer's response to Hegel's philosophy had another source. By identifying history as a process in which spirit realized itself, Hegel opened the way to modern philosophies in which humankind replaced God. Monotheism and humanism were both of them fictions, which acting together created the illusion that history contained some sort of redeeming significance. For Schopenhauer as for the Gnostics of ancient times, salvation was not an event in time but release from time. His philosophy was the polar opposite of modern Gnosticism, in which a self-deified humanity brings history to a triumphant conclusion.

In terms of the philosophers who came before him, Schopenhauer was a follower and critic of Kant. The great Enlightenment savant had demonstrated that reality was unknowable by human reason. All we have are phenomena – the world as it seems to us. How then should we live? A pious Christian, Kant could not accept the answer of David Hume, who advised a life guided by Nature, habit and convention. So Kant reinstated Christian values by way of rationalism. Any rational being that applied the categorical imperative – 'Act only according to principles you can accept as universal laws' – would come up with the same moral rules. This was, in effect, an Enlightenment reformulation of the Golden Rule, 'Do as you would be done by.'

Schopenhauer identified a flaw in this argument. Human beings who apply the Golden Rule do not come up with the same judgements of right and wrong. Christians who have done so have approved many practices now judged unjust – notably slavery. Kantians say this only shows the categorical imperative has been wrongly applied. But what reason is there for thinking it must yield a single set of universal laws? Unless a divine law-giver is assumed, there is no reason to think of ethics as obedience to any law. Schopenhauer thought the basis of ethics was in feeling – the emotion of compassion for others that may come with the realization that selfhood is an illusion. Salvation was the dissolution of this illusion. The liberated individual entered into a realm where the will is silent. Hints of this realm are glimpsed in moments when we are entranced by beauty. In thinking in this way, Schopenhauer was influenced by Indian philosophy – particularly the Vedantic school – which he was one of the first European thinkers to study.

Of the nature of this spiritual realm, Schopenhauer said nothing. Rejecting any idea of a creator-god, he was an uncompromising atheist. But when he insisted on the reality of something incommunicable he was not far from the apophatic theology of the German mystics and the Eastern Orthodox Church. In human terms this transcendent realm of pure being may seem like nothing at all. But the human mind is itself nothing, and in looking beyond itself it is seeking to pierce the veil of *maya* – universal illusion – and come nearer to reality.

Schopenhauer's mystical atheism inspired some interesting thinkers. One of them, now nearly forgotten, was the writer-philosopher Fritz Mauthner (1849–1923), author of a four-volume history of atheism. For Mauthner it was not belief in God that had to be given up by atheists but the idea of God itself. He considered some of the greatest mystics – such as the heretical German Meister Eckhart (1260–1328) who prayed to God to rid him of the idea of God – as atheists in this sense. The result of a thoroughgoing atheism was what Mauthner called 'godless mysticism' – the silent contemplation of a world beyond words. A radical nominalist who regarded our concepts as no more than useful tools, he believed language became deceptive when it dictated our view of the world. Unrecognized in philosophy aside from a dismissive remark in Wittgenstein's *Tractatus*, Mauthner's work had an enduring influence on Samuel Beckett, who for many years kept Mauthner's books at his bedside.[3]

Schopenhauer's thought has some limitations. He denounced the world as illusion, but nowhere explained how or why this illusion had come into being. His conception of salvation is no less problematic. If what lies behind the world is nothingness, the simplest path to salvation is suicide. Schopenhauer resists this implication with the argument that killing oneself solves nothing, since the will simply renews itself in some other form. But, if life is nothing but pain, death resolves everything for the suffering individual – however illusory he or she may be.

On the other hand, accepting that the world is an illusion need not mean seeking to escape from it. As Schopenhauer pictures it in much of his work, human life – like everything that exists – is purposeless striving. But from another point of view this aimless world is pure play. In some Indian traditions, the universe is the play (in Sanskrit, *lila*) of the spirit. Schopenhauer held fast to the belief that the world was in need of redemption. But from what? Everything that exists is only *maya*, after all. Seeking no deliverance from the world's insubstantial splendour, a liberated mind might find fulfilment by playing its part in the universal illusion.

TWO NEGATIVE THEOLOGIES: BENEDICT SPINOZA AND LEV SHESTOV

A clear line between atheism and negative theology is not easily drawn. An atheist who denies that any God created the world may affirm a God that permeates the world but about which little or nothing positive can be said. Believing that this immanent God could be known through the exercise of pure reason, while at the same time holding that it could be described only in negative terms, the seventeenth-century Dutch-Jewish philosopher Benedict Spinoza was such an atheist. Not a finite object but an infinite substance, subsisting eternally with no beginning or end in time, Spinoza's God was identical with the world and yet had none of the attributes of things in the world.

Spinoza begins the *Ethics*, his greatest work, aiming to show that

God must exist. By 'God' Spinoza means a single, infinite substance, *Deus sive Natura* – God or Nature. If God is understood in this way, the God of monotheism cannot exist. No transcendental power could have created the world, which is self-subsistent. The act of creation, in Jewish and Christian theology or myth, is an expression of free will. But whether in God or in human beings, free will is an illusion. The world is a universal system in which everything is as it must be. Nothing is contingent, and there are no miracles. In such a world the only possible freedom is freedom of mind, which means understanding that things cannot be otherwise than they are.

Denying even the logical possibility of a creator, Spinoza was an atheist of the most radical kind. Yet at the end of the *Ethics* he asserts that 'our salvation, or blessedness, or freedom, consists . . . in a constant and eternal love of God . . .' This 'intellectual love of God' is 'the highest good we can want' – the supreme good in human life. No one who understands God can hate God. But no one can ask God to love them in return, since they and God are not different things. Only one thing exists – God itself.[4]

It may seem strange that a thinker should seek to prove that the God of monotheism cannot possibly exist, and then go on to assert that love of God is the supreme good. What Spinoza is trying to do is bring into a single system of ideas two radically divergent ways of looking at the world – a view from an imaginary Absolute, necessarily infinite and eternal, and the view of a finite, mortal human individual. But these perspectives are too different to be compared, let alone melded into one.

Why Spinoza attempted this synthesis may become clearer once the context of his thought is explained. Born in 1632 in Amsterdam, where his family had fled from Portugal after Jews had been forced to convert to Christianity by the Inquisition, Spinoza had a traditional Jewish upbringing. Even as a youth he seems to have had doubts about the religion he was taught to follow. He made no attempt to convert his co-religionists to his views, but must have intimated some of the central themes of the *Ethics* to those around him. As a result he was excommunicated by the synagogue of Talmud Torah, the United Congregation of Portuguese Jews in Amsterdam, in 1656.

For the Jewish community that expelled him, Spinoza's hetero-doxy was not only a matter of doctrine but also an issue of security. Europe and the Netherlands were the site of intense religious contro-versies at the time, some of them violent, and conflict within or around Amsterdam's Jewish community could threaten its safety. Another reason for his expulsion may have been that Spinoza was in communication with other heterodox thinkers, some of them cov-ertly engaged in politics. What is undeniable is that Spinoza's thought was, in terms of Jewish and Christian orthodoxy, thoroughly heretical.

Following his excommunication Spinoza lived a quiet life, sup-porting himself as a lens-grinder. Aiming to be as independent as was practically possible, he refused an offer of an academic post because he believed his freedom might be compromised by holding such a position. He had no interest in wealth or possessions, and having secured his legal inheritance in a lawsuit against his stepsister renounced nearly all of it. In 1660 he left Amsterdam for a peaceful village near Leyden, staying in touch by correspondence with some of the greatest minds of the time, including the philosopher Leibniz and the scientists Huygens and Boyle. He spent his last years writing a treatise on politics, which he failed to finish. He died in 1677, prob-ably from complications of consumption from which he had suffered from his early years, a condition that his work as a lens-grinder may have exacerbated. Those who knew him spoke of him with affection, as a sweet-natured, courteous and modest person. His philosophy, on the other hand, was severe, unyielding and supremely ambitious.

In a letter, Spinoza declared: 'I do not presume to have discovered the best philosophy, but I know that I understand the true one.'[5] The rationalist philosophers of his time were all of them at odds with traditional religion, but they held back from challenging it directly. Descartes struggled with the mind–body problem, while Leibniz attempted to reconcile his rationalism with Christian orthodoxy. They were eager to respond to science, but not by abandoning monotheism.

More radical in his thinking, Spinoza broke with the most basic presupposition of monotheism – the dualism of mind and matter that underpins the idea that the world is God's creation. For Spinoza there could be only one substance, which was God itself. Sometimes described as pantheism – the belief that the universe itself is God – this is better understood as a version of Monism, in which the world is a single system, infinite and eternal.

Spinoza's philosophy dissolves many of the problems that come with monotheism. The problem of evil is removed by dispensing with the idea of evil as something independent of human beings. Since there is no free will, no one chooses to do or be evil. Good and evil are human attitudes to the world, not features of the world itself. For God or Nature there can be no evil.

One difficulty with this view of things is how Spinoza could know it to be true. He does not present it as having been verified by experience. That the world is a single infinite system was for him a necessary truth – a conclusion reached by pure reason. Spinoza's model for reason was mathematics – the *more geometrico*, or geometric method. Like the early Bertrand Russell, he believed that mathematics provided access to eternal truths. He never explained how the order of reason fitted with the world that is governed by physical laws. He was much inspired by the advancing sciences of his time, but his philosophy owed little to experimental methods of inquiry. His way of thinking had more in common with medieval scholasticism than with anything in modern science. Spinoza's argument that God exists by necessity is not very different from the so-called Ontological Argument presented by medieval Christian theologians such as St Anselm of Canterbury (1033–1109), which suggested that since the human mind contains the idea of a perfect being, such a being must exist. Like Anselm, Spinoza assumed an order in the cosmos that is reflected in the human mind. But the existence of any such order is an article of faith, not a conclusion that has been demonstrated by the use of reason. If the human mind mirrors the cosmos, it may be because they are both fundamentally chaotic.

Another question is why anyone should worship Spinoza's God. His vision of an infinite and eternal substance, lacking in anything that is contingent or accidental, has an austere grandeur. But it is only an intellectual construction, and why anyone should devote their life to such an abstraction is far from obvious. Spinoza tells us that one can only know God by setting aside any partial emotion or sympathy – any love one has for a particular person or place, for example. Again and again in his works, which were written in Latin, he enjoins the reader: *Non ridere, non lugere, neque destestari, sed intelligere* (Laugh not, weep not, be not angry, but understand). But it is not clear why anyone should immolate themselves on an altar built from metaphysical speculation. Why renounce our humanity for the sake of an indifferent Deity?

The Polish philosopher Leszek Kołakowski summarized Spinoza's philosophy as that of 'a resigned mystic, who clothed his personal mysticism in a Cartesian intellectual framework, a philosophy of escape, a theory of freedom attainable through the spiritual negation of the finite order of the world'.[6] But this hardly captures the ecstasy Spinoza imagines the fully rational human being experiencing when they understand that everything is as it has to be. Santayana, a great admirer of Spinoza's and a great critic of his philosophy, captured this state of mind when he wrote:

> By overcoming all human weaknesses, even when they seem kindly or noble, and by honouring power and truth, even if they should slay him, he entered the sanctuary of an unruffled superhuman wisdom, not because the world as he conceived it was flattering to his heart, but because his heart disdained all flatteries, and with a sacrificial prophetic boldness uncovered and relished his destiny, however tragic his destiny might be.

But, as Santayana goes on, the moral problem is not solved by Spinoza's self-identification with God or Nature. The finite soul may come to believe that it is part of a rational cosmos. But it is far from self-evident that any such cosmos exists: 'a really naked spirit cannot assume that the world is thoroughly intelligible. There may be surds, there may be hard facts, there may be dark abysses before which intelligence must be silent, for fear of going mad.'[7]

There are other tensions in Spinoza's thought. He has been read as a radical Enlightenment thinker who promoted a far-reaching version of liberalism.[8] It is true that he was not only an impassive metaphysician. He was also an impassioned partisan of freedom of inquiry and expression. But what is the point of these freedoms if human beings cannot think otherwise than they do? If the only possible freedom is understanding your place in a necessary scheme of things, a slave can be free. This was the view of the Stoic philosopher Epictetus (AD 50–135), himself born a slave. If they were more rational and had better control of their passions, Epictetus believed, slaves could be freer than their masters. But Spinoza did not imagine that most of humankind would ever become rational beings. In his writings on politics he is explicit that much of humanity cannot grasp truth and must be governed through the use of myths and symbols. He goes so far as to say that they ought not to read him: 'the multitude, and those of like passions with the multitude, I ask not to read my book; nay, I would rather that they should utterly neglect it, than that they should misinterpret it after their wont.'[9]

In this Stoic–Spinozist view liberal freedoms can have only an indirect value for the mass of humankind. Nor can they have much value for the few who are rational, who will be as free living under tyranny as they would be in a liberal regime. Political and social liberty, which was at the heart of Spinoza's liberalism, fades into insignificance in the larger context of his thought. The only freedom that matters is inner freedom, which – according to Spinoza – consists in the acceptance that everything in the world is as it must be.[10]

The end-result of Spinoza's philosophy is that freedom is submission to necessity. This was the conclusion reached by the Russian-Jewish religious thinker Lev Shestov (1866–1938), who rejected Spinoza's philosophy for this reason. An uncompromising rationalist, Spinoza believed that God could be known only through the exercise of pure reason. Shestov was a fideist of the most radical kind. Not only did he think faith was independent of reason. He believed that God was reached only by breaking the bounds of reason. God was a realm of infinite possibility lying beyond all laws, whether of logic or ethics.

No two modern philosophers are as opposed in their views of God and freedom as Spinoza and Shestov. For Shestov, Spinoza was the prophet of a fatal illusion. His aim was to contain all the world in a single system of necessary truths. But this left no room for spiritual freedom. Spinoza's philosophy imprisoned the soul in a conceptual gaol the human mind had built for itself. Yet Shestov seems to have loved Spinoza, regarding him as his indispensable antagonist and most cherished interlocutor.

According to Shestov, every human conception of God had to be relinquished. Here he resembled the heretical medieval mystic Meister Eckhart. In both thinkers the distinction between the creator and the human soul is blurred, sometimes to the point that it disappears altogether. If Eckhart must be described as an atheist, as Mauthner claimed, so must Shestov.

In his magnum opus *Athens and Jerusalem* Shestov wrote:

> The power of the biblical revelation – what there is in it of the incomparably miraculous and, at the same time, of the absurdly paradoxical, or, to put it better, its monstrous absurdity – carries us beyond the limits of all human comprehension and of the possibilities that comprehension admits. God: this means that there is nothing that is not impossible . . . fallen man aspires, in the final analysis, to the promised 'nothing will be impossible for you'.[11]

For Shestov, it is the nature of faith to demand the impossible. Spinoza, on the other hand, demanded submission to necessity because he was bewitched by an idea of unity:

> We live in narrowness and injustice. We are obliged to press close to each other, and in order to suffer the least possible, we try to maintain a certain order. But why attribute to God, the God whom neither time nor space limits, the same respect and love for order? . . . There is no need at all. Consequently the idea of total unity is an absolutely false idea. And as philosophy cannot ordinarily do without this idea, it follows therefore, as a second consequence, that our thought is stricken with a terrible malady of which we must rid ourselves, no matter how difficult it may be.[12]

Spinoza's philosophy was, for Shestov, an example of this malady. He shared with Spinoza the belief that God transcends all human attributes. Otherwise they could hardly be more different.

In some ways Shestov is closer to Santayana than he is to Spinoza. As has been seen, Santayana rejected Spinoza's belief that the world must be finally intelligible. 'This world is contingency and absurdity incarnate,' Santayana wrote, 'the oddest of possibilities masquerading momentarily as fact.'[13] Shestov agreed, but drew quite different conclusions. For Santayana, contingency – the arbitrary, accidental nature of the world – was a predicament to be escaped. For Shestov, boundless contingency was God incarnate.

It was not only in Spinoza that Shestov found a philosophy of submission to necessity. The same idea was expressed in Nietzsche's superman, who finds freedom in *amor fati* – the love of necessity. (Interestingly, when Nietzsche refers to Spinoza in his writings it is always with admiration.) Spinoza and Nietzsche were both in thrall to Greek philosophy. Both worshipped fate, not God.

A lifelong reader of Dostoevsky, the subject of two of his early books,[14] Shestov sides with the underground man in his rebellion against the 'crystal palace' of reason. Like Ivan Karamazov, Shestov rejected any kind of theodicy. Faith was not a search for harmony, but rebellion against any system of thought that aimed to reconcile humankind with necessity. He mocked the attempt to find any sense or logic in history:

> People seek the meaning of history, and they find it. But why must history have a meaning? The question is never raised. And yet if someone raised it, he would begin, perhaps, by doubting that history must have a meaning, then continue by becoming convinced that history is not at all called to have a meaning, that history is one thing and meaning another.[15]

Shestov spoke from experience. Born in Kiev and growing up in a circle of brilliant Russian thinkers and writers, he watched Russia disintegrate during and after the First World War and then fall under Bolshevik repression. He left Russia in 1919 after a period of university teaching in Kiev, when he was instructed to add a Marxist preface to a book he had completed on religious themes. He refused, and after a long and arduous journey reached Paris, where he spent the rest of his life. His writings attracted interest far beyond the intellectuals of the Russian diaspora. The French atheist thinker Georges Bataille, the Romanian-French essayist Emile Cioran, Albert Camus and D. H. Lawrence (who contributed a foreword to an English translation of Shestov's *All Things are Possible*)[16] were among those who admired his work.

Shestov's thought intrigued many of his contemporaries but found few followers. He had only one disciple. The Romanian-Jewish poet, film-maker and essayist Benjamin Fondane (1898–1944) was attracted to Shestov, whom he met in Paris in 1924 and for whom he later worked as an assistant, for his assault on reason. Like Mauthner, Fondane was acutely aware of the limitations of language. His poetry, much of it Symbolist in style, was an attempt to point beyond words.[17] He loved silent films because the absence of speech made them more expressive. A film in which he was himself involved, *Rapt*, flopped because it contained very little sound at a time when talkies were already dominant.

Shestov's observation that history is one thing, meaning another, is illustrated in the life of his disciple. With the outbreak of the Second World War Fondane joined the French army. In a letter to his sister at the time, he wrote: 'Better to perish if the universe knows no gods other than Hitler.' After being captured by the Germans he escaped and spent some time in hospital suffering from appendicitis. Despite efforts by friends to secure him passage to New York or Argentina, he spent the rest of the war in hiding in Paris, without income or papers and refusing to wear the yellow badge prescribed for Jews. In March 1944 he was found and arrested by the French police and sent to Drancy, the site of a processing centre for the death camps. Fondane's friends appealed to the Romanian legation – where the cultural attaché at the time was the playwright Eugene Ionesco – and his release was secured. But Fondane's sister's freedom could not be guaranteed, and he refused to leave without her. His sister's fate is not known, but it seems likely that she perished in a later deportation.

On 30 March Fondane was sent to Auschwitz-Birkenau. According to reports by survivors, he spent as much of his time as he could in animated philosophical discussion with other prisoners. He seems to have known that he was marked out to be murdered. In October, weeks before Soviet soldiers liberated the camp, he was gassed.[18]

In a short piece in memory of Fondane, Cioran – who claimed to have tried to warn his friend to change residence more often since otherwise he could be betrayed by a concierge – remembered him with vivid affection:

> The most creased and furrowed face one could imagine, a face with millennial wrinkles never still, animated as they were by the most contagious and the most explosive torment: I could not contemplate that countenance enough. Never before had I seen such harmony between experience and utterance, between physiognomy and speech.[19]

According to Cioran, Fondane was indeed betrayed to the police by his concierge. He seemed untroubled about his safety – 'a strange "unconcern" on the part of someone who was anything but naïve, and whose psychological and political judgements testified to an exceptional perspicacity'.[20] Perhaps Fondane believed that only a miracle could save him.

Fondane's teacher also wanted to live in a world in which miracles occurred. Shestov came to faith by way of radical doubt. But sceptical doubt, however radical, cannot bring the unlimited freedom Shestov demanded. What he wanted was to return to things as they were before the Fall, when all things seemed possible. But the Fall is the price of consciousness. There is no way back.

Conclusion

LIVING WITHOUT BELIEF
OR UNBELIEF

The God of monotheism did not die, it only left the scene for a while in order to reappear as humanity – the human species dressed up as a collective agent, pursuing its self-realization in history. But, like the God of monotheism, humanity is a work of the imagination. The only observable reality is the multitudinous human animal, with its conflicting goals, values and ways of life. As an object of worship, this fractious species has some disadvantages. Old-fashioned monotheism had the merit of admitting that very little can be known of God. As far back as the prophet Isaiah, the faithful have allowed that the Deity may have withdrawn from the world. Awaiting some sign of a divine presence, they have encountered only *deus absconditus* – an absent God.

The end-result of trying to abolish monotheism is much the same. Generations of atheists have lived in expectation of the arrival of a truly human species: the communal workers of Marx, Mill's autonomous individuals and Nietzsche's absurd *Übermensch*, among many others. None of these fantastical creatures has been seen by human eyes. A truly human species remains as elusive as any Deity. Humanity is the *deus absconditus* of modern atheism.

A free-thinking atheism would begin by questioning the prevailing faith in humanity. But there is little prospect of contemporary atheists giving up their reverence for this phantom. Without the faith that they stand at the head of an advancing species they could hardly go on. Only by immersing themselves in such nonsense can they make sense of their lives. Without it, they face panic and despair.

According to the grandiose theories today's atheists have inherited from Positivism, religion will wither away as science continues its advance. But while science is advancing more quickly than it has ever done, religion is thriving – at times violently. Secular believers say this is a blip – eventually, religion will decline and die away. But their angry bafflement at the re-emergence of traditional faiths shows they do not believe in their theories themselves. For them religion is as inexplicable as original sin. Atheists who demonize religion face a problem of evil as insoluble as that which faces Christianity.

If you want to understand atheism and religion, you must forget the popular notion that they are opposites. If you can see what a millenarian theocracy in early sixteenth-century Münster has in common with Bolshevik Russia and Nazi Germany, you will have a clearer view of the modern scene. If you can see how theologies that affirm the ineffability of God and some types of atheism are not so far apart, you will learn something about the limits of human understanding.

Contemporary atheism is a continuation of monotheism by other means. Hence the unending succession of God-surrogates, such as humanity and science, technology and the all-too-human visions of transhumanism. But there is no need for panic or despair. Belief and unbelief are poses the mind adopts in the face of an unimaginable reality. A godless world is as mysterious as one suffused with divinity, and the difference between the two may be less than you think.

Acknowledgements

This book has benefited enormously from the thoughts of my editors and friends. Simon Winder, my editor at Penguin, has improved the text greatly, and it has been much enhanced by suggestions from Eric Chinski, my editor at Farrar, Straus and Giroux. Adam Phillips has given the book immense encouragement, together with many detailed comments which helped me frame how I wanted to write it. Tracy Bohan has nurtured the book all though its passage from conception to publication. I am grateful to her and her colleagues at the Wylie Agency for their unfailing support.

The book has been enriched by conversations with a number of people over the years. Among them I would like to thank Bryan Appleyard, Robert Colls, Henry Hardy, Bas Heijne, David Herman, Gerard Lemos, Michael Lind, James Lovelock, Pankaj Mishra, Alan Ponter, Paul Schütze, Will Self, Geoffrey Smith, Nassim Taleb and Marcel Theroux. Reading and talking with the late Norman Cohn had a formative impact on my thinking about religion and politics.

None of these people bears any responsibility for the use I have made of their thoughts and observations.

My greatest debt of gratitude is to my wife Mieko, without whom the book would not have been written.

John Gray

Notes

INTRODUCTION: HOW TO BE AN ATHEIST

1. Robin Lane Fox, *Pagans and Christians*, London, Penguin Books, 2006, 31–2.
2. William Empson, *Seven Types of Ambiguity*, London, The Hogarth Press, 1984, 1, 11.

CHAPTER 1: THE NEW ATHEISM: A NINETEENTH-CENTURY ORTHODOXY

1. L. Wittgenstein, *Remarks on Frazer's Golden Bough*, ed. Rush Rhees, trans. A. C. Miles, Corbridge, Brynmill Press, 2010, 8.
2. Richard Robinson, *An Atheist's Values*, Oxford, Oxford University Press, 1964, 9.

CHAPTER 2: SECULAR HUMANISM, A SACRED RELIC

1. For a detailed discussion of medieval millenarianism and modern politics, see my book *Black Mass: Apocalyptic Religion and the Death of Utopia*, London, Penguin Books, 2008.
2. Catherine Nixey, *The Darkening Age: The Christian Destruction of the Classical World*, London, Macmillan, 2017, xxxvii.
3. Bertrand Russell, *The History of Western Philosophy*, New York, Simon & Schuster, 1945, 364.
4. See Gareth Stedman Jones, *Karl Marx, Greatness and Illusion: a life*, London, Allen Lane, 2016, 'Postscript: A Note on Marx and Judaism', 165–7.
5. See Jonathan Sperber, *Karl Marx: a nineteenth-century life*, New York, Liveright, 2013, 421.
6. John Stuart Mill, *Essential Writings*, ed. with an introduction by Max Lerner, New York, Bantam Books, 1961, 31, 34.
7. Ibid., 89–90.

8. Ibid., 81.

9. Ibid., 13–14.

10. Ibid., 98.

11. I added to the enormous philosophical literature on Mill myself in my book *Mill on Liberty: a defence*, London, Routledge, 1983, 2nd edn 1996; 2nd edn republished in Taylor & Francis e-library, 2003.

12. Alexander Herzen, *My Life and Thoughts*, trans. Constant Garnett, introduction by Isaiah Berlin, Berkeley, University of California Press, 1999, 463.

13. *John Stuart Mill on Liberty and Other Essays*, ed. John Gray, Oxford, Oxford University Press, 1998, 140.

14. Ibid., 15.

15. John Stuart Mill, *Nature and the Utility of Religion*, ed. George Nakhnikian, Indianapolis and New York, Bobbs-Merrill, 1958, 64–5.

16. Henry Sidgwick, *Methods of Ethics*, 7th edn, Indianapolis and Cambridge, Hackett, 1981, 508.

17. For a more extended discussion of Sidgwick's philosophy and his involvement in psychical research, see John Gray, *The Immortalization Commission: science and the strange quest to cheat death*, London, Penguin Books, 2012. The purported posthumous text from Sidgwick is cited on p. 43.

18. Bertrand Russell, *Autobiography*, vol. 1: *1872–1914*, London, George Allen & Unwin, 1967, 146.

19. Bertrand Russell, *Autobiography*, vol. 2: *1914–1944*, London, George Allen & Unwin, 1968, 38.

20. Bertrand Russell, *Sceptical Essays*, London, Routledge, 2004, 13.

21. Bertrand Russell, *The Practice and Theory of Bolshevism*, New York, Harcourt, Brace & Howe, 1920, 20, 117.

22. Russell, *Autobiography*, vol. 1, 209.

23. Sidgwick allowed for a measure of reasonable hypocrisy, but only if it could be justified by universal principles. On Sidgwick's defence of an 'esoteric morality', see Gray, *The Immortalization Commission*, 57–8.

24. Michel Onfray, translated by Jeremy Leggatt, *In Defence of Atheism: the case against Christianity, Judaism and Islam*, London, Serpent's Tail Books, 2007, 34.

25. F. Nietzsche, *Twilight of the Gods and The Anti-Christ*, trans. with an introduction and commentary by R. J. Hollingdale, London, Penguin Books, 1968, 131.

26. Ibid., 163.

27. Ayn Rand, *We the Living*, 2nd edn, New York, Signet Books, 1959, viii.

28. Ayn Rand, *We the Living*, New York, Macmillan, 1936, 92–4.

29. See Michael Prescott, 'Romancing the Stone-Cold Killer: Ayn Rand and William Hickman', michaelprescott.typepad.com.

30. See Bernice Glatzer Rosenthal, *Nietzsche in Russia*, Princeton, Princeton University Press, 1986, for a useful overview of Nietzsche's impact on Russian art and thought.

31. I was told of the impact of Rand's cigarette-holder on her audiences by a former Randian believer.

32. See Murray Rothbard, 'The Sociology of the Ayn Rand Cult', rothbard.altervista.org.

33. Lucretius, *On The Nature of the Universe*, trans. Ronald Melville with an introduction by Don and Peta Fowler, Oxford, Oxford University Press, 1997, 36.

CHAPTER 3: A STRANGE FAITH IN SCIENCE

1. H. G. Wells, *Anticipations*, London, Chapman & Hall, 1902, 317. I discuss Wells's views more fully in *The Immortalization Commission: the strange quest to cheat death*, London, Penguin Books, 2012, 131.

2. *The Autobiography of Charles Darwin*, New York, Barnes & Noble, 2005, 67.

3. Charles Darwin, *On the Origin of Species*, Ware, Wordsworth Editions, 1998, 368.

4. T. H. Huxley, 'Evolution and Ethics', Romanes Lecture, 1893, alepho. clarku.edu/huxleyCE9/E-E.html.

5. These passages from Hume and Kant are cited by Richard H. Popkin in 'Hume's Racism', in Richard H. Popkin, *The High Road to Pyrrhonism*, ed. Richard A. Watson and James E. Force, Indianapolis and Cambridge, Hackett, 1993, 254–5, 259–60.

6. Popkin, *The High Road to Pyrrhonism*, 81.

7. Voltaire, *Philosophical Dictionary*, London, J. and H. L. Hunt, 1824, vol. 1: *Atheism*, 328.

8. For a comprehensive study of Enlightenment anti-Semitism, see Arthur Hertzberg, *The French Enlightenment and the Jews: the origin of modern anti-Semitism*, New York, Schocken Books, 1968.

9. Peter Gay, *The Party of Humanity: essays in the French Enlightenment*, New York, Knopf Doubleday, 1964, 351–4.

10. I refer here to Carl Becker's *The Heavenly City of the Eighteenth-Century Philosophers*, New Haven and London, Yale University

Press, 2004. First published in 1932, this remains the best book on the Enlightenment.

11. For an illuminating study of Mesmer's life and work, see Vincent Buranelli, *The Wizard from Vienna*, London, Peter Owen, 1976.

12. Ibid., 183.

13. Among those who compared Mesmer with Freud was the Austrian writer Stefan Zweig. See *Zweig's Mental Healers: Franz Anton Mesmer, Mary Baker Eddy, Sigmund Freud*, first published in 1932 by the Viking Press, New York, republished by Plunkett Lane Press, Lexington, Mass., 2012. I argued against the view of Freud as a psychological healer in *The Silence of Animals: on progress and other modern myths*, London, Penguin Books, 2013, 83–96.

14. Leon Trotsky, *Literature and Revolution*, https://www.marxists.org/archive/trotsky1924/lit_revo/index.htm.

15. Leon Trotsky, *The Defence of Terrorism*, London, Labour Publishing Company, 1921, 60.

16. C. S. Lewis, *The Abolition of Man*, New York, HarperCollins, 2001, 65.

17. J. B. S. Haldane, 'Daedalus; or, science and the future', https://www.marxists.org/archive/haldane/works/1920s/daedalus.htm.

18. Yuval Noah Harari, *Homo Deus: a brief history of tomorrow*, London, Harvill Secker, 2016, 46.

19. Ibid., 46.

20. Henry Sidgwick, *Methods of Ethics*, 7th edn, Indianapolis and Cambridge, Hackett, 1981, xx.

21. Ray Kurzweil, *The Singularity is Near: when humans transcend biology*, London, Penguin Books, 2005, 389.

22. The transhumanist philosopher Nick Bostrom has become fearful of the dangers that further advances in artificial intelligence will bring. See his book *Superintelligence: paths, dangers, strategies*, Oxford, Oxford University Press, 2014.

CHAPTER 4: ATHEISM, GNOSTICISM AND MODERN POLITICAL RELIGION

1. Norman Cohn, *The Pursuit of the Millennium: revolutionary millenarians and mystical anarchists of the middle ages*, revised and expanded edn, New York and Oxford, Oxford University Press, 1970, 15.

2. Eric Voegelin, *Science, Politics and Gnosticism*, with an introduction by Ellis Sandoz, Washington, Del., ISI Books, 2004, 64–5.

3. Hans Jonas, *The Gnostic Religion: the message of the alien God and the beginnings of Christianity*, Boston, Beacon Press, 1963, 42–5.

4. Cohn, *The Pursuit of the Millennium*, 281.

5. Alexis de Tocqueville, *L'Ancien Régime et la Revolution*, Bk 1, Chapter iii, cited by Carl L. Becker, *The Heavenly City of the Eighteenth-Century Philosophers*, New Haven and London, Yale University Press, 2004, 154–5.

6. Cited in Becker, *The Heavenly City of the Eighteenth-Century Philosophers*, 157–8.

7. Nicolas Berdyaev, *The Origin of Russian Communism*, London, Geoffrey Bles, 1937, 9.

8. Robert Service, *Lenin: a biography*, London, Macmillan, 2000, 365.

9. Lesley Chamberlain, *The Philosophy Steamer: Lenin and the exile of the intelligentsia*, London, Atlantic Books, 2006.

10. Donald Rayfield, *Stalin and his Hangmen*, London, Penguin Books, 2005, 82.

11. See George Leggett, *The Cheka: Lenin's political police*, Oxford, Oxford University Press, 1971, 178.

12. I have discussed the God-builders in John Gray, *The Immortalization Commission: the strange quest to cheat death*, London, Penguin Books, 2012, where Krasin's speech is cited on p. 161.

13. Ibid., 169.

14. Friedrich Percyval Reck-Malleczewen, *Diary of a Man in Despair*, trans. Paul Rubens with an introduction by Norman Stone, London, Duckworth, 2000, 30–32. Reck-Malleczewen's study of Bockelson has been published in English under the title *A History of the Munster Anabaptists: inner emigration and the Third Reich. A critical edition of Friedrich Reck-Malleczewen's Bockelson: a tale of mass insanity*, ed. and trans. George B. von der Lippe and Victoria M. Reck-Malleczewen, New York, Palgrave Macmillan, 2008.

15. Reck-Malleczewen, *Diary of a Man in Despair*, 229.

16. See Michael Burleigh, *The Third Reich: a new history*, London, Pan Books, 2000, 4–5.

17. For an illuminating presentation of links between German policies towards the Herero and Nama peoples and the Holocaust, see Edwin Black, 'In Germany's Extermination Programme for Black Africans, a Template for the Holocaust', *The Times of Israel*, 5 May 2016.

18. I refer chiefly to the German historian Ernst Nolte, who systematically effaced the specifically German origins of Nazism, denied the

uniqueness of the Holocaust and copied Nazi rhetoric by arguing that Jews made themselves targets because some of them had participated in communist movements. See Ernst Nolte, *Three Faces of Fascism*, London, Weidenfeld & Nicolson, 1965.

19. Arthur Koestler, *Arrival and Departure*, London, Jonathan Cape, 1943, 42–4. I discussed Nazi modernism in *Al Qaeda and What It Means to be Modern*, London, Faber & Faber, 2003 and 2007, 11–16.

20. John Stuart Mill, *Auguste Comte and Positivism*, Ann Arbor, University of Michigan Press, 1973, 141, 170.

21. See Stanislav Andreski, *Social Sciences as Sorcery*, London, Penguin Books, 1975.

CHAPTER 5: GOD-HATERS

1. Cited in Simone de Beauvoir, 'Must We Burn Sade?', in *The Marquis de Sade: an essay by Simone de Beauvoir*, with selections from his writings chosen by Paul Dinnage, London, New English Library, 1972, 9.

2. Ibid.

3. Cited by Geoffrey Gorer in *The Life and Ideas of the Marquis de Sade*, London, Peter Owen, 1934, revised and enlarged edn, London, Panther Books, 1964, 21.

4. Cited in ibid., 25.

5. Ibid., 44.

6. The Marquis de Sade, *Dialogue between a Priest and a Dying Man*, in *Three Complete Novels and Other Writings*, New York, Grove Press, 1966, 173–5.

7. Cited by de Beauvoir, 'Must We Burn Sade?', 41.

8. Ibid., 42.

9. Ibid., 39.

10. The Marquis de Sade, *Juliette*, Grove Press, New York, 1968, 309.

11. Ibid., 411.

12. The Marquis de Sade, *The 120 Days of Sodom and Other Writings*, New York, Grove Press, 1967, 364.

13. Sade, 'Philosophy in the Bedroom', in *Three Complete Novels and Other Writings*, 319.

14. Ibid.

15. Sade, *Juliette*, 732.

16. Ibid., 772.

17. Sade, *The 120 Days of Sodom*, 72–3.

18. Theodor Adorno and Max Horkheimer, *Dialectic of Enlightenment*, trans. John Cumming, London, Verso Books, 1979, 118.

19. Nikolai K. Mikhailovsky, 'Dostoevsky's Cruel Talent', in Fyodor Dostoevsky, *Notes from Underground*, ed. and trans. Michael R. Katz, New York, W. W. Norton, 2001, 142.

20. Dostoevsky, *Notes from Underground*, 23–5.

21. Ibid., 25.

22. Fyodor Dostoevsky, *Winter Notes on Summer Impressions*, trans. Richard Lee Renfield with a foreword by Saul Bellow, New York, McGraw-Hill, 1965, 90–91.

23. Fyodor Dostoevsky, *Demons*, trans. and annotated by Richard Pevear and Larissa Volokhonsky, London, Vintage Books, 2006, 617–19.

24. Ibid., 402.

25. Ibid., 404–6.

26. Fyodor Dostoevsky, *The Brothers Karamazov*, trans., introduced and annotated by Richard Pevear and Larissa Volokhonsky, London, Vintage Books, 2004, 245.

27. Albert Camus, *The Myth of Sisyphus*, London, Penguin Books, 2005, 103.

28. Dostoevsky, *Demons*, 616.

29. Dostoevsky, *The Brothers Karamazov*, 258–62.

30. Ibid., 649.

31. L. Shestov, *All Things are Possible*, trans. S. S. Koteliansky with a foreword by D. H. Lawrence, London, Martin Secker, 1920, 81.

32. Dostoevsky, *The Brothers Karamazov*, 245.

33. Vasily Rozanov, *Dostoevsky and the Legend of the Grand Inquisitor*, trans. with an afterword by Spencer E. Roberts, Ithaca and London, Cornell University Press, 1972, 115.

34. William Empson, *Milton's God*, Cambridge, Cambridge University Press, 1981, 260.

35. Ibid., 268.

36. Ibid., 251.

37. Ibid., 260.

38. Ibid., 259.

39. For an illuminating examination of dualistic religions and heresies, see Yuri Stoyanov, *The Other God: dualist religions from antiquity*

to the Cathar heresy, New Haven and London, Yale University Press, 2000.

40. Empson, *Milton's God,* 248.
41. Ibid., 250.
42. Ibid., 246.
43. Ibid., 251.
44. Ibid., 255.
45. Ibid., 249.
46. Ibid., 251–2.
47. I discuss the Aztecs at greater length in *The Soul of the Marionette,* London, Penguin Books, 2016, 73–90.
48. Empson, *Milton's God,* 62.
49. Ibid., 64, 65.
50. William Empson, *The Face of the Buddha,* ed. Rupert Arrowsmith, Oxford, Oxford University Press, 2016.
51. William Empson, *The Complete Poems,* ed. with an introduction and notes by John Haffenden, London, Penguin Books, 2001, 3.
52. William Empson, *The Structure of Complex Words,* Chatto & Windus, London, 1951, 421.
53. Empson, *Milton's God,* 246.
54. Nicolas Berdyaev, *The Destiny of Man,* New York, Harper & Brothers, 1960, 26.

CHAPTER 6: ATHEISM WITHOUT PROGRESS

1. Cited in Anthony Woodward, *Living in the Eternal: a study of George Santayana,* Nashville, Tenn., Vanderbilt University Press, 1988.
2. John McCormick, *George Santayana: a biography,* New York, Paragon House, 1987, 391.
3. Cited in Woodward, *Living in the Eternal,* 110.
4. McCormick, *George Santayana,* 370–71.
5. See ibid., 471–2, 504.
6. 'On my Friendly Critics', in George Santayana, *Soliloquies in England and Later Soliloquies,* with a new introduction by Ralph Ross, Ann Arbor, University of Michigan Press, 1967, 246.
7. George Santayana, *Three Philosophical Poets,* New York, Doubleday, 1953, 183.
8. George Santayana, *Dominations and Powers: reflections on liberty, society and government,* Clifton, NJ, Augustus M. Kelley, 1972, 17–20.

9. Santayana, *Soliloquies in England*, 251.

10. Santayana, *Dominations and Powers*, 462.

11. Ibid., 94.

12. Ibid., 340.

13. George Santayana, *Platonism and the Spiritual Life*, New York, Charles Scribner's Sons, 1927, 3.

14. Ibid., 231–2.

15. For Santayana's critique of Russell, see George Santayana, 'The Philosophy of Bertrand Russell', in *Winds of Doctrine*, New York, Harper Torchbooks, 1957, 138–54.

16. Marcel Proust, *Remembrance of Things Past*, vol. 1: *Swann's Way*, trans. C. K. Scott Moncrieff, London, Vintage Classics, 1966, 51.

17. George Santayana, *Scepticism and Animal Faith*, New York, Dover Publications, 1955, 75.

18. For a discussion of Santayana's debts to Samkhya philosophy, see Woodward, *Living in the Eternal*, 98–101.

19. George Santayana, *Realms of Being: one-volume edition with a new introduction by the author*, New York, Cooper Square, 1972, 741–2.

20. Santayana, *Platonism and the Spiritual Life*, 89.

21. Ibid., 85.

22. Ibid., 312.

23. Jeffrey Meyers, *Joseph Conrad: a biography*, London, John Murray, 1991, 115.

24. Ibid., 51, 115.

25. Cited in Cedric Watts, *A Preface to Conrad*, 2nd edn, London and New York, Longman, 1993, 7.

26. Joseph Conrad, 'An Outpost of Progress', in Joseph Conrad, *The Nigger of the Narcissus and Other Stories*, ed. J. H. Stape and Allen H. Simmons with an introduction by Gail Fraser, London, Penguin Books, 2007, 235–6.

27. See Meyers, *Joseph Conrad*, Chapter Sixteen, Appendices 1 and 2.

28. G. Jean-Aubry, *Joseph Conrad: life and letters*, vol. 1, London, Heinemann, 1927, 141.

29. Ian Watt, *Conrad in the Nineteenth Century*, Berkeley, University of California Press, 1979, 139.

30. Bertrand Russell, *The Autobiography of Bertrand Russell*, vol. 2: *1914–1944*, London, George Allen & Unwin, 1968, 161.

31. Cited in Watts, *A Preface to Conrad*, 57.

32. Ibid., 48.

33. Joseph Conrad, *The Shadow Line*, Oxford and New York, Oxford University Press, 1992, xxxvii–xxxviii.

34. Joseph Conrad, *Victory: an island tale*, with an introduction by John Gray and notes and appendix by Robert Hampson, London, Penguin Books, 2015, 408.

35. Watts, *A Preface to Conrad*, 65.

36. Ibid., 80.

37. Ibid., 78.

38. Ibid., 342.

39. Arthur Schopenhauer, *The World as Will and Representation*, vol. 1, trans. E. F. J. Payne, New York, Dover Publications, 411–12.

40. Bertrand Russell, *The Autobiography of Bertrand Russell*, vol. 1: *1872–1914*, London, George Allen & Unwin, 1967, 9.

41. Cited in Watts, *A Preface to Conrad*, 76–7.

42. Joseph Conrad, *The Nigger of the Narcissus*, ed. with an introduction by Jacques Berthoud, Oxford and New York, Oxford University Press, 1984, 90.

CHAPTER 7: THE ATHEISM OF SILENCE

1. Arthur Schopenhauer, *The Wisdom of Life and Counsels and Maxims*, New York, Prometheus Books, 1995.

2. Arthur Schopenhauer, *Parerga and Paralipomena: short philosophical essays*, vol. 2, trans. E. F. J. Payne, Oxford, Clarendon Press, 393.

3. I discuss Mauthner in *The Silence of Animals: on progress and other modern myths*, London, Penguin, 2013, 138–46. A comprehensive study of Mauthner's work can be found in Gershon Weiler's *Mauthner's Critique of Language*, Cambridge, Cambridge University Press, 1970.

4. Benedict de Spinoza, *Ethics*, ed. and trans. Edwin Curley with an introduction by Stuart Hampshire, London, Penguin Books, 1996, 176–7, 169.

5. Quoted in Stuart Hampshire, *Spinoza and Spinozism*, Oxford, Clarendon Press, 2005, 23.

6. L. Kołakowski, 'The Two Eyes of Spinoza', in *Spinoza: a collection of critical essays*, ed. Marjorie Green, New York, Anchor Books/Doubleday, 1973, 286.

7. George Santayana, 'Ultimate Religion', in *The Philosophy of George Santayana*, ed. with an introductory essay by Irwin Edman, Random House, New York, 1936, 587–8.

8. See Jonathan Israel, *Radical Enlightenment: philosophy and the making of modernity, 1650–1750*, Oxford, Oxford University Press, 2001.

9. Benedict de Spinoza, *A Theologico-Political Treatise and A Political Treatise*, trans. from the Latin by R. H. M. Elwes with a bibliographical note by Francesco Cordasco, New York, Dover Publications, 1951.

10. There may be parallels between Spinoza's idea of inner freedom and some eastern religious traditions. For a comparison with Zen Buddhism, see Paul Wienpahl, *The Radical Spinoza*, New York, New York University Press, 1979.

11. Lev Shestov, *Athens and Jerusalem*, trans. with an introduction by Bernard Martin, New York, Simon & Schuster, 1968, 69.

12. Ibid., 431–2.

13. George Santayana, *The Sense of Beauty*, London, Constable, 1922, 142.

14. Lev Shestov, *Dostoevsky, Tolstoy and Nietzsche: the Good in the teaching of Tolstoy and Nietzsche*, trans. Bernard Martin, and *Dostoevsky and Nietzsche: the philosophy of tragedy*, trans. Spencer Roberts, with an introduction by Bernard Martin, Athens, Ohio, Ohio University Press, 1978.

15. Shestov, *Athens and Jerusalem*, 393.

16. Leo Shestov, *All Things are Possible*, authorized translation by S. S. Koteliansky with a foreword by D. H. Lawrence, London, Martin Secker, 1920.

17. For a collection of Fondane's poetry, see *Cinepoems and Others*, ed. Leonard Schwarz, New York, New York Review Books, 2016.

18. I am indebted for details of Fondane's life and death to Bruce Baugh's Introduction to *Existential Monday: philosophical essays*, ed. and trans. Bruce Baugh, New York, New York Review of Books, 2016, vii–xxxv.

19. E. M. Cioran, 'Benjamin Fondane, 6 Rue Rollin', in *Anathemas and Admirations*, trans. Richard Howard, New York, Arcade Publishing/ Little, Brown, 1991, 218.

20. Ibid., 220.